DES Daughter

I was little more than thirteen years old and anxiously waiting for my periods to start. It was a time of great excitement. Many of my friends at school had already had their first periods; they seemed to have taken a great step in life, and I didn't want to be left too far behind.

Well, the day finally arrived. It was one evening after school, and I was ready for it.

"Ma, Ma, come here!" I called.

My mother knew immediately why I was calling. She had been ready for this momentous event. Coming into my room, she smiled softly as she gently slapped both my cheeks and then hugged me. "That's so you will always have rosy cheeks," she explained. "My mother did it to me, and now I've done it to you."

I was a little startled by Mom's ceremonial gesture but I also felt proud. I couldn't wait to get to school the next morning so that I could casually tell my friends that I was a woman now, too.

At the time, I could never have suspected that this so-called honor would be with me for only a brief five years.

DISCARDED

DES

DAUGHTER

THE JOYCE BICHLER STORY

JOYCE BICHLER

 AVON
PUBLISHERS OF BARD, CAMELOT AND DISCUS BOOKS

DES DAUGHTER is an original publication of Avon
Books. This work has never before appeared in book
form.

Cover photograph by Tatiner/Gamma/Liaison

AVON BOOKS
A division of
The Hearst Corporation
959 Eighth Avenue
New York, New York 10019

Copyright © 1981 by Joyce Bichler
Published by arrangement with the author
Library of Congress Catalog Card Number: 80-69917
ISBN: 0-380-78147-6

First Avon Printing, July, 1981

AVON TRADEMARK REG. U.S. PAT. OFF. AND IN
OTHER COUNTRIES, MARCA REGISTRADA, HECHO EN
U.S.A.

Printed in the U.S.A.

10 9 8 7 6 5 4 3 2 1

**To my mother and father,
who have always given me
their love and support.**

ACKNOWLEDGMENTS

I would like to thank my editor [illegible] responsible for the [illegible] tion of the importance of [illegible] ability to write [illegible] ing its development [illegible]

I also want [illegible] reasons goes [illegible] and [illegible] gave me the [illegible] book is for all [illegible]

Finally, to M[illegible] with my typewriter [illegible]

ACKNOWLEDGMENTS

I would like to thank my editor, Jean Feiwel, who is responsible for the existence of this book. Her recognition of the importance of this story, her belief in my ability to write it, and her guidance and assistance during its development turned the improbable into reality.

I also want to thank everyone who for a variety of reasons goes unmentioned in the book. Your presence and caring during the hard times medically and legally gave me the courage to fight back on both levels. This book is for all of you.

Finally, to M.L.K. who kept me locked in the study with my typewriter until the last chapter was written.

PART ONE

PART ONE

CHAPTER 1

I was little more than thirteen years old and anxiously waiting for my periods to start. It was a time of great excitement. Many of my friends at school had already had their first periods; they seemed to have taken a great step in life, and I didn't want to be left too far behind.

Well, the day finally arrived. It was one evening after school, and I was ready for it.

"Ma, Ma, come here!" I called.

My mother knew immediately why I was calling. She had been ready for this momentous event. Coming into my room, she smiled softly as she gently slapped both my cheeks and then hugged me. "That's so you will always have rosy cheeks," she explained. "My mother did it to me, and now I've done it to you."

I was a little startled by Mom's ceremonial gesture, but I also felt proud. I couldn't wait to get to school the next morning so that I could casually tell my friends that I was a woman now, too.

At the time, I could never have suspected that this so-called honor would be with me for only a brief five years.

From the time I was quite young I knew I would be going to college. It was just one of those things that I never questioned. Neither of my parents had gone to college. My mother is a full-time housewife and my father a New York City firefighter. But I had always done very well in school, and my parents expected me to continue. That was fine with me. I had really enjoyed school, and now, at age seventeen, I was proud to be

11

graduating from the Bronx High School of Science. It was one of those high schools that had an entrance exam that you had to pass for admission. The academic standard is fairly high, and I had done fairly well in all of my classes. Socially, however, matters were a little more disappointing. I had lots of friends (mostly female) but no boyfriends or anything even close to that. I definitely wanted to continue my studies, but I also had high hopes that college would bring an improvement in my social life.

Now the time had come. After anxiously checking the mail for weeks, I finally got a letter of acceptance from the State University of New York at Stony Brook. It was a fine school: It had high academic standards, it was strong in the sciences, and it wasn't too far from home. The perfect choice. My parents were still uneasy about me leaving the nest but were also pleased that I had decided on Stony Brook.

Going away to college was a big event for me. I had never been away from home for more than a day or two before. Even now I was only going fifty miles away, but I would be living there. On campus. On my own. The thought was scary, exciting, and challenging.

I had been so protected at home. The youngest child, I was very much the baby of the family since my brother, Dennis, was nine years older, and my sister, Arlene, was twelve years older than I. My mother seemed blind to the fact that I had grown up, and continued to treat me like the baby. She worried whenever I went out with friends and had to ride the subway (she'd read the day's crime report to me as I walked out of the house); she worried that I didn't wear warm enough clothes whenever the temperature dropped below 50; and she worried if I didn't get home at exactly the time I said I would. Three years away from twenty, I felt like an adult and couldn't understand why my mother didn't treat me as such. I loved her but frequently felt insulted by her actions.

Now, with college in sight, life at home became particularly difficult. Arlene and Dennis were both married and out of the house, and it was hard for my parents to accept the fact that I too would be leaving home soon. They were trying, though, and during those last few weeks, I was as tactful and cooperative as possible. But I could still see how tough it was for them.

Anyway, I made the break without too many tears, and, in fact, my mother was able to direct her concerns into the task of sending me weekly supplies of roast chickens, soup, and canned goods, which would arrive regularly, without fail. In sending these "Care packages," Mom was still taking care of me. I didn't complain; I enjoyed the food.

In the meantime, I was trying to cope with the academic life of college. I had made the decision to go bio-premed (which, in retrospect, came from watching too much "Dr. Kildare" and "Medical Center" in my early years), and although I had always been an A student in high school, the shock of Chemistry and Calculus 101 was too much for me. Everyone else in my class seemed so bright, and extremely competitive, and it was a struggle to keep up with the volume of the work, particularly in math, which had always been a difficult subject for me. I felt I was in over my head. I was scared that I would lose confidence in my academic abilities and flunk out. But I hung on and managed not to panic too much.

I might not have been at the top of the class, but I was really beginning to enjoy the social side of college. As I have said, I had hardly known any boys in high school, but now, suddenly, all these guys were interested! It was wonderful. Even some of the people I had gone to high school with and who had never noticed me before were now asking me out. This puzzled me a lot. I even went so far as to believe it was because I had had my hair professionally straightened just before going to Stony Brook. (Its natural state is a permanent

13

frizz.) I enjoyed being a student. I was making new friends, learning to be a little more independent, building up my confidence, and generally becoming very excited by life. Despite the strain of some of my classes, I loved college.

Toward the end of September I heard that there was to be a Beach Boys concert held at the university. I was a great fan and arranged to go with my friend, Rosey, her boyfriend, Stuie (whom I had not met), and their friend Michael (whom I also had not met).

I felt as though I already knew Stuie because Rosey had told me so much about him. When he came to pick us up for the concert, I greeted him as if I had known him for years. As Michael followed quickly behind, I felt I couldn't just give him a little "Hi, Mike" after I'd been so friendly to Stuie, so I gave him an enthusiastic greeting as well. It certainly made Mike notice me! Michael Lewis Kimbarow was eighteen, tall, slim, dark, and easy to talk to. We both came from the Bronx and even had some friends in common. He was not a student. He had dropped out of college that year and was working in a men's clothing store in New York at the time. He was charming and friendly, and I liked him. We had a terrific time at the concert that evening and Mike invited himself back up for another visit the following week. I wasn't sure about that. I was glad he was interested but felt rather uncomfortable about it. I didn't want to be pushed in any direction.

Mike did come up the next week, but I spent quite a bit of time avoiding him and seeing my regular friends. I was annoyed and alarmed when Mike seemed to want to "get into my pants." I just wasn't ready for that, and after Mike's second visit I decided that whatever potential our relationship might have had, it was now all over.

Rosey, however, had other ideas. My work was beginning to get the better of me. The more I struggled with my chemistry, the more upset I became; my efforts seemed to lead me nowhere. Noticing my gloom, Rosey suggested that we go home for a weekend in the Bronx (where she also lived), and relax and take it easy.

"And while you're there, why don't you and Mike come out with Stuie and me?" she asked casually while we were getting washed up in the dorm bathroom.

"Mike? Does he still want to go out with me?" I was amazed.

"He sure does. He's been asking about you!"

"I really would like to see him again." I felt rather guilty for having been so aloof from him on his last visit.

We all met up in New York that weekend and had a wonderful time together. (I discovered that Stuie, with similar matchmaking tactics, had persuaded Mike that I was equally eager to go out with him!) I realized that I was very attracted to Mike, and he came to realize that I still needed time to think about a physical relationship, and did not push me.

Before long, Mike and I had worked out a weekend relationship, seeing each other either in New York City on my trips home, or at Stony Brook when he came out to visit. This arrangement worked well, and we became very close very fast. I was certainly falling for him, but I still remained fairly cautious because he seemed so unsettled. Having dropped out of college, he still didn't know what direction he was going in. But he was warm, sensitive, and terribly handsome. Best of all, we enjoyed each other's company and had lots of fun together.

CHAPTER 2

Apart from being in love and struggling desperately with chemistry and calculus, I suddenly had something else on my mind. Since I had started college I had noticed that my periods had become very irregular. Instead of having four days of bleeding, it was more like seven or eight. My menstrual cycle seemed to be completing itself every three weeks instead of four, and the bleeding was lasting longer and longer.

For the first few months I kept thinking that my menstrual cycle had been upset by all the recent changes in my life. After all, I had just left home for the first time, I was leading a typically irregular student life, and I was in love. It was easy to rationalize but not easy to forget about, though I did my best not to be bothered by it.

By the time I went home for the Christmas break, Mike and I had become very attached to each other. I had met and liked his parents, and Mike had been to my house several times. My parents seemed to like him a lot. More important was the fact that Mike had become clearer about what he wanted to do. He had decided that he definitely did want to finish college and was planning to go to night school in January while continuing to work at the clothing store. He hoped to quickly become a matriculated student and then return to school full time.

I had been doing some thinking about my own future and had decided to drop the idea of becoming a doctor. I had seen the reality of studying for it and did not want to dedicate my entire life to medicine. Meanwhile, I had become very interested in sociology and wanted to take a few courses in that area to see what it was like. I decided to avoid plunging into things too quickly.

Everything seemed to be falling into place at last—everything, that is, except my health. By December, I had no weeks between periods at all: I was bleeding almost constantly. I was going through a jumbo-sized box of tampons in just ten days. I still tried not to be alarmed. I still told myself that this irregularity was caused by the changes in my life, and that it would eventually get back to being normal all by itself. But much as I tried to deny it, the fear was there. I was terrified that there was something seriously wrong with me. I just wasn't ready to face it yet.

I hid the box of tampons in the back of my closet so my mother wouldn't notice how quickly they disappeared.

By the time I returned to school in January I was practically hemorrhaging. The bleeding was so profuse I could no longer even try to ignore it. I was frightened, and I knew I had to do something. Urged by Mike and Rosey, I finally called the university's health services clinic to make an appointment to see a doctor. At first the secretary told me that the clinic was so busy I would have to wait six weeks before there would be an opening, but after I had described my symptoms I was told to come in the next day.

That night I couldn't sleep. I lay in bed worrying. Part of me was sure something was seriously wrong, and part of me was hoping desperately that everything would be all right. Finally, frustrated by my inability to sleep, I turned on the light and picked up a magazine to read. Unlike me, my roommate was still on the bio-premed course, and she always left medical journals lying around. I enjoyed flipping through them occasionally, and I hoped that this one would induce me to sleep. I turned the pages, only to discover an article

17

about cervical cancer. To my horror, it described the exact symptoms I had—in particular, the ever-increasing bleeding. Unable to read any further, I threw the journal on the floor. Cancer? I could not believe that could happen to me. How could it? Why me? What a cruel coincidence that I should come across that journal at this time.

I spent the rest of the night falling in and out of a fitful sleep and miserably recalling the haunting words of that article. Tomorrow, I thought, I'll know for sure.

I was up and dressed early in the morning and ready to walk over to the health clinic for my examination. I was very nervous and spent at least half an hour pacing up and down my room before it was time to leave. I was going to the clinic alone. I would have liked having someone to accompany me, but everyone had classes that morning and couldn't skip them to wait with me.

It only took a few minutes to walk from my dorm to the clinic, but during that time I realized that I was actually more frightened about the internal exam than anything else. I had never had one before, though friends of mine had. An internal exam is one of those things about which those who have already had it say, "It doesn't hurt." But there was always something in the way they said it that made me a little skeptical. In fact, I was not frightened of any pain that I might experience; I just didn't really want anyone poking around inside me like that.

Once I had checked in at the clinic, I was told to take a seat and wait. And wait I did. I knew the clinic was busy, but I hadn't expected the delay to be this long. I wished I had a friend with me to talk to. I tried to read the magazines on the table or focus on the television, but nothing helped to alleviate my anxiety. The longer I waited, the more anxious I became until I really felt I could hardly bear it. I felt nauseous from worry.

After I had been sitting in the waiting room for two hours a nurse finally called "Joyce Bichler." I jumped up from my chair, only to discover that I now had to sit in the hallway to wait some more. If I hadn't been so tense, I would have become angry, but instead I felt helpless. I wanted to get in there to see the doctor and get it over with, but at the same time I would have been just as happy to run out of the door and forget the whole thing.

After another half an hour I was called into the small examination room. "Undress completely," said the nurse, "and put this on." She handed me a paper dressing gown. "Doctor Borg will be with you soon." She went out.

I undressed and waited, naked under my gown. After fifteen minutes, the doctor walked in. I was so relieved to see a woman in that white coat. Somehow that made a tremendous difference. She was in her thirties, slim with brown hair tied up on her head. I knew it would be easier to talk to another woman about my body than to a man.

Dr. Borg questioned me about my symptoms. When I told her about the extent of my bleeding, she didn't seem too concerned. That's a good sign, I thought.

Now for the internal exam. Dr. Borg's assistant, who had come in with her, told me to climb up onto the high examining table and lie back with my buttocks near the end, my legs up. I felt extremely undignified in this position and could feel my heart thumping. The assistant, a friendly, soft-spoken woman, told me to relax as the doctor started the examination.

When Dr. Borg inserted the speculum, the unexpected coldness of the metal made me jump. "You're all right, this doesn't hurt," she said.

There was a feeling of pressure inside me, but no pain. I was grateful for that, and relaxed a little.

"Now I'm going to do a Pap test," Dr. Borg said as she removed the speculum. My muscles involuntarily tensed up. This is bound to hurt, I thought. I was getting uncomfortable having these instruments inside me, particularly since I couldn't see what was going on.

But it was soon over, and without any pain. The doctor seemed very calm. She wrote down a few notes.

"It's probably an infection of some sort," she said. "Take these vaginal suppositories and follow the directions. And make an appointment to see me again in a week."

The doctor seemed unconcerned by what I had told her and what she had seen. I felt a little sheepish about my fears of the previous night. I certainly wasn't going to mention the article on cervical cancer if she thought that the only thing wrong with me was an infection. I didn't need to bring up the subject at all. I was so happy I could have kissed her and her assistant. I dressed, picked up my prescription, and practically danced out of there.

Back at the dorm I was in such good spirits I couldn't help boasting. I was one of the few there who had had an internal exam. I told my interested audience that it was nothing and that it hadn't hurt a bit. Everyone was pleased. I even called up Mike to tell him the good news. He seemed to be almost as relieved as I was. Everything was okay.

I had to insert the suppositories twice a day, morning and evening. They were yellow, wedge-shaped, and waxy, and they came with a plastic applicator. They were easy enough to insert, but I hated having to lie there afterward while they dissolved into what felt like a gooey mess. They made me feel so dirty, but I told myself that if they were going to clear up the infection and get rid of this horrible bleeding, I could put up with them.

Unfortunately, the suppositories seemed to have no effect at all—even after four days. The bleeding had only become worse; the flow was constant and heavy.

My feelings of relief and happiness quickly turned into anxiety. I was desperate for the week to end so that I could see the doctor again. I decided that this time I wouldn't be so scared and I'd ask more questions to find out what was really going on. I also now knew that until I found out the results of the Pap test, I couldn't truly rest easy.

Probably because of all the recent stress I had been under, I suddenly became severely ill with the flu. It was on the weekend, and Mike was visiting. The flu was the last thing I needed. I had already missed a day of classes that week by going to the doctor and now I would miss more because I was so sick. Having changed my major to social sciences, I had been doing well academically and I didn't want to fall behind. But there was little I could do. The flu hit me hard. I ran a fever, I was congested, I ached all over, and I felt very weak. I just crawled into bed and felt sorry for myself. My friends were solicitous and frequently checked that I was all right, and on Sunday Mike decided to stay an extra day to care for me.

My appointment with Dr. Borg was for the next day, Monday. I woke up that morning feeling worse than ever. I couldn't conceive of how I would make it down to the clinic.

"Call for an ambulance," Mike suggested. "That can get you to the clinic and then you can also see what they'll do for your flu."

"But I'm not that sick," I protested. "No, I'll call Dr. Borg and see what she has to say about my Pap test. Then I'll schedule another appointment."

Mike was by my side as I dialed the clinic's number. Dr. Borg was busy, but I was put through to her assistant, who said she remembered me. I explained my situation to her and she said she would talk to Dr. Borg and be right back.

I could feel my heart beating as I waited for her to

21

return. A few minutes later she was back on the phone. "The Pap came back negative, you'll be pleased to hear," she said. "Just continue using the suppositories until they are used up. Dr. Borg doesn't want to see you again until three months from now."

Sick as I was, I could have jumped up and down when I got off the phone. Mike and I hugged each other with happiness. I felt as if a great burden had been lifted from my shoulders. Deep down I felt that everything was going to be all right. I had just panicked, that was all.

Mike returned to the city that afternoon, content with the knowledge that the flu was the most serious thing wrong with me. Some hours after he had left, I got out of bed to go to the bathroom. As I crossed the hall, I felt a gush of blood running down my leg like nothing I'd ever felt before. I dashed into the bathroom, but it was too late. The sight of the vivid, glistening trail of blood shocked me. I felt as though I were hemorrhaging. My peace of mind hadn't lasted long. Miserable, I cleaned up the blood from the floor. Tomorrow I would call the doctor again and ask her about the bleeding.

I called Dr. Borg first thing the next day. I told her I was worried because I was bleeding so much, and she gave me an appointment for the next week. It seemed like a long time, but at least I would have a chance to get rid of my flu. I was now listless and depressed and more scared than I'd ever been.

During that week's wait, I recovered from the flu but the bleeding was constant. Mike was now very concerned too and shared my anxiety over this next visit.

The next week, at the clinic, I went through the waiting ritual again. After a few hours I was finally carted into an examining room, but to my surprise there was another young female patient also waiting to see the doctor. I asked what she was there for and she explained that she was seeing Dr. Borg about birth control. I was very puzzled.

Finally, Dr. Borg arrived and without pausing she started to describe the physical characteristics of the cervix, uterus, and vagina, and how the diaphragm works. I couldn't believe it. I was dumbfounded. But not for long. As Dr. Borg gave both of us diaphragms to hold and look at, a surge of desperate feeling gave me language. "I am *not* here for a birth control lecture," I said loudly. "I want some medical attention." I stared at the doctor and could feel my hand shaking as it held the diaphragm. In fact, Dr. Borg looked pretty flustered herself as she ushered the other woman into the room next door, saying that she would be back soon to look at me.

I sat there, alone, waiting for the doctor to return. I was rapidly losing confidence in this woman. I was really starting to wonder about her.

After fifteen minutes she returned. She explained that she had thought I had come to be fitted for a diaphragm, that it was a misunderstanding. Practically in tears, I told her that was not the case and that, as I had told her on the phone, I was still bleeding. Before I could think about a diaphragm, I wanted the bleeding to stop. The suppositories hadn't helped and I wanted something done.

"Let's give this another look," the doctor said calmly. Her calmness was beginning to annoy me; she seemed too casual. Off came my clothes and on went the paper dressing gown. I climbed onto the examining table, legs up. Dr. Borg's assistant came to watch over her shoulder this time. I was bleeding so heavily that it took a few minutes for the doctor to swab away the blood before they could get a clear view of my cervix. Once that was done, then they did react to what they saw. The two of them began muttering to each other. I could feel my heart beating uncomfortably. I heard the doctor ask her assistant if she saw that "cut." Cut? How could I get a cut on my cervix?

The examination was over and I got dressed. The doctor told me that I had a cut on my cervix that needed suturing. She said that they could not do it at the clinic because they did not have the right facilities but that she was sending me to a Dr. Collier, whose office was in the town of Stony Brook. She gave me his number and told me to call for an appointment. She sounded so brusque and matter-of-fact that I was too scared to ask what suturing was. She might have known that something was wrong, but was being calm to soothe me. I just didn't know. Clutching the piece of paper with Dr. Collier's number, I walked the short distance to my room in a daze.

Rosey and my roommate, Marlene, were a great comfort to me that week. Rosey explained that suturing meant stitching and did her best to make me look on the bright side of things. After all, at least I now knew what it was. My Pap had been negative; the bleeding was coming from a cut that might just have been caused by tampons, we speculated. The only thing I had to worry about now was whether it would hurt when they stitched the cut.

I spent hours on the phone with Mike every evening. He was wonderful about everything—understanding, concerned, and comforting. I felt very close to him.

While it was easy to talk to Mike about all this, I was not yet ready to tell my parents anything. They worried about me even when there was nothing wrong. I decided that if I told them at all, it would be when all this was over and I was completely back to normal. I felt guilty about not telling them, but I knew it was the best policy at that point.

I had made an appointment to see Dr. Collier the following week, but there was a problem. Dr. Collier's office was off campus and since I and my friends were freshmen, none of us had a car. I did know a few sophomore guys who had cars but I was too embarrassed to ask any of them to drive me to a gynecologist. In the end I decided to use the student volunteer ambulance corps, which provided transportation for students who had appointments with off-campus doctors. I had a late-afternoon appointment, so there would be no rush, and Marlene said that she would accompany me. We were all set.

The day of the appointment I spent the morning in a state of nervousness. I could not concentrate on my work; I kept thinking about what the suturing would be like. But the hours did pass, and Marlene and I got to the ambulance with time to spare.

The ambulance took us over to the small medical complex in the middle of suburban Stony Brook. Stony Brook is a quaint old town on the north shore of Long Island. Its residents, many of whom are well-to-do, all share a dislike for the university students. Stony Brook, despite having high academic standards, was also known for its rowdiness.

I don't know if it was my nervous state or what, but as soon as Marlene and I walked into the doctor's office I could feel all eyes turned on us. We were obviously students from the university and I must have looked so scared that I'm sure they all thought I was pregnant—and single.

The office was small and packed. Everyone looked married, upper-middle-class, and very pregnant. I made my way up to the desk where the receptionist sat. She was a large woman, with a deep, loud voice. She wasn't very friendly. She asked for my name, which I told her. Then she said that since I hadn't been to the office before, she needed more information. In a booming voice she first asked me if I was married or unmarried, and then if I was there for birth-control information. It was obvious that she thought I was pregnant. I don't know why I was so embarrassed, but I felt that everyone in the waiting room was listening and also unfairly dismissing me as one of those "irresponsible students."

Marlene and I took our seats and waited. We didn't talk much to each other and the minutes dragged by. Waiting at the clinic on campus seemed like nothing compared to this. And there we were, surrounded by fat, rich, pregnant women. I felt very out of place.

It was dark outside when my name was called. Marlene gave me a reassuring look and wished me good luck. I took a deep breath.

The examining room was much larger and brighter than the one at the university. The nurse gave me a dressing gown. I undressed and waited for the doctor to arrive.

Dr. Collier came in. He was middle-aged and thin, and had a very pleasant face. "Now then," he said, "what can we do for you?" He sounded very friendly. I explained briefly to him why I was there.

"Well," he said, "I'd better have a look at you." I assumed what had come to be a hated position—on my back, legs in the stirrups, eyes staring at the blank ceiling. I felt totally vulnerable. Dr. Collier was chatting to me as he inserted the speculum. I didn't really hear what he was saying. All I could hear was my heart beating. There was silence as the doctor peered between my legs. "My God," he suddenly shouted. "You look like chopped meat in there!"

I don't remember much of what happened after that. My head was spinning, the room was going around and around and everything looked hazy. Suddenly Dr. Collier was standing over my head. "Where on earth did you have the abortion?" he demanded angrily. I was sobbing uncontrollably. "Tell me, Miss Bichler, *where* did you have the abortion?" His tone was suddenly softer.

I couldn't believe his question. "I didn't have an abortion," I blurted out through my tears.

26

"Come now, it's obvious that you've had an abortion. And whoever did it made a good mess. You can trust me. Tell me where you had it."

It was several minutes before I finally convinced Dr. Collier that I had not had any abortion. He looked as shocked as I felt. I don't remember the rest of the examination.

I don't remember getting dressed or walking from the examining room to Dr. Collier's office, but soon I was sitting by his desk, crying hysterically and using up handfuls and handfuls of tissues. Through my tears I saw him drawing diagrams as he explained the type of surgery he would be doing on me. I heard him saying that he had taken a biopsy and that I had a serious problem with my cervix. He was saying that he would be doing a conical operation to remove a portion of my cervix. None of this could sink in properly. My head was still spinning. I just stared at the pictures he kept drawing. I heard him say he didn't want me to go back to my dorm room, that my condition was too serious for that. He was saying he wanted me in the hospital immediately. Then he asked if my parents knew that I had come here. That did sink in. My sobbing became louder. "It's time they knew," the doctor said kindly.

I didn't argue. I was simply a little girl just turned eighteen. At that moment there was nobody I wanted with me more than my mother and father. I cried even harder at the thought of telling them. How would my mother react to this hysterical doctor telling her I had to go into the hospital immediately?

I told Dr. Collier I couldn't stop crying long enough to call my mother.

"I'd better do it, then," he said. He still looked quite shaken himself. I wrote down my home phone number, and he dialed.

"Hello, Mrs. Bichler? This is Dr. Collier from Stony

Brook. . . . Just a second, calm down. . . . Yes, she is ill. . . . Hello? Hello?"

Mom has passed out.

I was crying so loudly I couldn't hear most of what Dr. Collier was saying. He seemed to be talking to my sister, Arlene, who happened to be at our parents' house. When she saw my mother pass out, she quickly picked up the telephone. There was much discussion back and forth, but I missed it all.

The next moment Dr. Collier was off the phone. "Your parents are going to call their doctor in the city to hear what he has to say," he said. He looked distressed as he muttered, "Why do people always think doctors in New York City are better than those in the suburbs?"

Ten minutes later, Dr. Daniel from New York called. (He was my sister-in-law's gynecologist.) Dr. Collier had a brief conversation with him. It seemed that Dr. Daniel had decided that my condition was not in need of immediate hospitalization. He told Dr. Collier that he would call my parents back and tell them so.

Only a few minutes after that, my sister called Dr. Collier to tell him they would be coming to pick me up back at my dorm room. She asked Dr. Collier to give me the biopsy sample he had taken so that I could give it to Dr. Daniel when I saw him. Then she wanted to speak to me. The thought of my parents coming to rescue me had cheered me up a bit. I took the phone. "Hello."

"Hello, Joyce? Are you okay?" Arlene sounded concerned and in control.

"Oh, yes, I'm fine," I said. I found myself trying to sound happy.

"Joyce, what's going on?" Arlene asked. "You're not pregnant, are you?"

I was stunned for a second. "No!" I almost shrieked into the phone. I started to cry again. Arlene told me to calm down and said that I should go back to my dorm and pack. They would be there in an hour. She asked if I wanted Michael to be there. I said, "Yes, very much so."

After we had hung up, I said my goodbyes to Dr. Collier. He asked me to let him know how things went. I felt as though I had been in that room for days.

When I walked back into the waiting room, a woman who had been sitting there for hours waiting for the doctor just glared at me. I must have been a sight! My eyes were red and I was still whimpering. My friend Marlene ran up to me. She could tell something was terribly wrong. I told her what had happened inside the office. She was really very comforting, and I tried to be reassuring. I tried to hold back my fears. Somehow we had to get back to the dorm. The receptionist was still very hostile, particularly now, since I had completely screwed up the doctor's schedule, but she reluctantly let Marlene use the telephone to call the ambulance service. Marlene was told that the ambulance would be there in ten minutes. We gathered up our coats and decided to wait outside the office. We both still felt very uncomfortable with all the stares we were getting from the other patients.

It was too cold to wait outside so we sat on a milk bucket in the hallway just outside the door to the waiting room. We waited and we waited. I was not feeling too great. In fact, I felt faint. Marlene began to get nervous. After half an hour, Marlene went back to call the ambulance service again. She was told that they were on their way and that we should be patient.

After another fifteen minutes I was getting upset. I knew my parents were on their way and I didn't want them to arrive to pick up their sick daughter, only to discover I wasn't there. Luckily, Marlene had already called Rosey at the dorm. (My friends had all been waiting anxiously for our return and had become a little panicked when we had been gone for so many hours.) Marlene assured me that if my parents did arrive before us, then someone would definitely tell them that we had been delayed at the doctor's.

The ambulance still hadn't come. I began to feel desperate. I went back into the doctor's office, and called the service myself. I practically screamed at the person at the other end of the phone. I said that they had to pick me up right away because I was seriously ill.

The ambulance did finally arrive. It turned out that they were late because one of the drivers had been giving a driving lesson to a new volunteer and had forgotten to take the walkie-talkie with him, so that he couldn't be contacted until the lesson was over. When I heard this, I was convinced that I was having a nightmare. It was unbelievable.

We managed to get back to the dorm before my parents had arrived. Marlene and I walked into our room and there were all our friends. Since Marlene's call to Rosey, they had cleaned our room so that it would look respectable for my parents. I think it was the only way they felt they could be useful in the situation. I was touched, but they all looked so grim. I didn't know what Marlene had told them but thought she must have laid it on thick.

Within a few minutes my parents arrived with my sister and her husband, Bob. Behind them came Michael. None of us talked very much, but as soon as they came I felt I had to cheer up and not show how scared I was. I knew that they would be strong if I was strong. My mother was in tears and my father looked very distressed. Arlene was in control and helped me gather my things together. I could tell she was working hard at trying to be calm. Mike was friendly, keeping conversation going with everyone, giving me meaningful looks. I couldn't bear to see my parents so upset, so I packed quickly, taking enough clothes for about a week.

It was time to say goodbye to all my friends. I'll never forget their faces—it was as though I were going off to die. They were trying to cheer me up and they all said they'd visit but they looked sad. I hugged Rosey and then Marlene very tight. I knew I would miss them all.

We packed ourselves into the car—six of us in a Buick Skylark. It was my father's car, but he must have been very shaken because it was my brother-in-law, Bob, who was driving. I had with me the record album I had bought for Mike's birthday, which was in a few days. I silently handed it to him in the car. Poor Mike, everyone's tension seemed to be focused on him. It was as if the family were convinced that whatever my problems, they had to be his fault in some way. They didn't include him in their conversations. Ironically, it was I who tried to make some cheery comments, but nothing went over very well so I kept quiet for most of the ride, as did everybody else.

Once home, I was able to escape with Mike into my bedroom. It was there that I felt most comfortable talking to him. I explained frankly what had happened in the doctor's office. When I had finished, Mike was clearly upset, but I was happy that I had been able to talk openly to him about it. With my family I just had to be brave. My brother, Dennis, and his wife, Helene, soon arrived. Dennis is always the joker, and he helped to alleviate the tense atmosphere that evening.

After the visitors had gone home that night, I was finally left on my own. I climbed into bed and cried. I had put up a front all evening, but now I couldn't deny what had happened. I was so frightened. I was convinced that I had cancer. I knew about cancer. My father had had to deal with this disease during the previous years. Approximately eight years earlier he had suddenly developed cancer of the kidney and had had to have one of his kidneys removed. I was only ten years old when my father went into the hospital. I remembered all of the whispering that went on in the house so that I wouldn't hear. That only alarmed me more. I would act brave during the day but cried myself to sleep every night until my daddy came home from the hospital. I remembered how much he had suffered when recovering from the surgery. A few years after that he had developed cancer of the bladder. It was not a spread of the kidney cancer but was another primary site. That surgery was easier, because the doctor had only to cut away the small area with the tumor, but I vividly remembered my father's pain. So cancer was not unfamiliar in our household, but that didn't make it any less frightening. Whatever support I was being given by my family and friends, ultimately I would be alone. That was a terrifying realization. But now I began to focus my fears on the fact that again no one would tell me what was wrong. I was to see Dr. Marc Daniel the next day and I was going to make sure that he gave me some straight answers.

The next day I went to Dr. Daniel with my mother, my father, and my sister. Michael had to work that day and I was to call him after I had seen the doctor.

Doctor Daniel's office, in an apartment building on a main street in the Bronx, was about a ten-minute drive from where my parents lived. It was a Wednesday, and Dr. Daniel didn't have office hours on Wednesday. He was seeing me now only because Dr. Collier had reported my condition as being so serious.

Empty of patients, the office had an eerie atmosphere. When I met Dr. Daniel, I was convinced that it would not work out. A large, tall man, Dr. Daniel was in his sixties. He was intent and serious, without much of a bedside manner, and he spoke in a constant growl. There were no comforting words from him on meeting. We all waited for him while he poked around in his examining room for a few minutes until he came back to say that he would not be able to examine me there. The nurse wasn't on duty, he said, and the equipment wasn't prepared. He made a few calls and then explained that he would examine me in one of the treatment rooms of Lebanon Hospital—only a few blocks away.

Within a few minutes we were in Lebanon Hospital in a large, bare examining room. My family waited outside in the hall while Dr. Daniel examined me. I was lying on my back again as he looked inside me. This time there were no comforting words or screams about chopped meat. He was silent, and took his time. After examining me, he asked me a lot of questions about my personal life in a tone that made them sound like accusations. His seeming lack of compassion also made me feel quite hostile toward him.

Before long, the doctor told me to get dressed and come with my family into the office next door. There I handed Dr. Daniel the biopsy sample that Dr. Collier had taken. He said he wanted to get the results of the biopsy and at that time could better determine what was going on.

All at once we started questioning him.

"What do *you* think is wrong with Joyce, Doctor?"

"When will you have the results of the biopsy?"

"Do you think it's really serious?"

"What," asked my sister, "if the sample isn't benign. What if it's malignant?"

At this Dr. Daniel flushed with rage. "Do *not* use the word *malignant!*" he shouted at Arlene. "It isn't going to be malignant."

Arlene looked stunned. We were all startled, but rage took me over. "Don't you yell at my sister like that!" I screamed, as tears came to my eyes again. "I want to know if it *is* cancer. I don't want you to forbid the use of any words, none at all. I can handle it, and I don't want any cover-ups. Don't be afraid of using the word *cancer*."

My whole family was now in tears. Dr. Daniel had evidently had enough of us. He rose from his chair and shunted us out of the office. He would call as soon as the biopsy results came in, he said coldly. Probably Friday. Meanwhile, he said, I was to stay at home.

Once home, I told my mother that I didn't like Dr. Daniel and that I didn't want to continue with him. I thought he was too old and stuffy. I couldn't talk to him and I didn't trust him. I was convinced he would not be the kind of doctor that would be honest with me. Honesty was becoming very important. Mom said that we should wait until the biopsy report came in. Then we could decide if I wanted to continue with him. She said she liked him because he was older and she felt he had lots of experience. "Anyway," she said, "perhaps the biopsy will be negative and then everything will be okay. You won't need to go to any doctor."

I didn't believe her. Gloom hung heavy in the air, though Mike managed to cheer me up a little when he came over that evening. He was so much easier than anyone else to talk to about what was happening to me.

The next day, Dr. Daniel called. He asked my mother if she had taken any medications while she was pregnant with me. I happened to be sitting in the same room and heard my mother's end of the conversation clearly. Mom said yes, she definitely remembered taking something during her pregnancy with me. She could not remember what it was. All she knew was that the obstetrician had given her a medication to "help save the baby." She had stained during the first three months and he had given her some pills to prevent her from miscarrying. The doctor, she said, a Dr. Fleischer, was still practicing, although he was by now a very old man. She took a few minutes to flip through her address book to give Dr. Fleischer's phone number to Dr. Daniel. When my mother got off the phone she was quite agitated. "Dr. Daniel thinks that a medication I took when I was pregnant with you might have something to do with the problems you're having now," she said. I didn't say anything. That was so long ago. I didn't see how there could be such a connection.

Poor Mom. She was so perturbed that she decided to call Dr. Fleischer herself to see what medication it was.

Within a few minutes she had Dr. Fleischer on the phone and had explained the situation to him. Dr. Fleischer said he would be glad to look up his records for her. After a long pause he came back on the phone and said that according to his records he had prescribed the drug DES to her. It was a drug called diethylstilbestrol. The obstetrician said he hoped this information was helpful and that everything would be okay.

CHAPTER 3

The next day, Friday, the biopsy report came in. My mother received the call from Dr. Daniel. He said he wanted me to go to the hospital as soon as a bed was available. The biopsy was positive and further tests had to be done. I was to go into Albert Einstein College Hospital. A bed would not be available until Monday—Washington's Birthday. The information was heard but not registered. I was functioning instinctively, automatically, and that's how I would cope with each day.

It got very cold that weekend. There was a terrible ice storm in the city. Sunday was Mike's birthday. It was his first birthday since we had met. In spite of everything, we were determined to have a good time. We decided we would go to a Chinese restaurant on Fordham Road.

We took the bus most of the way and then had to walk down a hill to get to the restaurant. The street was a solid sheet of ice and we slid the whole way there. It really made us laugh, and helped to release a lot of the tension we both felt.

At our table in the restaurant, Mike and I talked about what the next few weeks might bring. Our earlier exuberance had gone. I felt uncomfortable sitting there knowing I had a cancer growing inside me. I still couldn't really believe it, but we spoke of the possibility of surgery, of a hysterectomy, and how that might change my life. Mike kept telling me how much he loved me; that made us both want to cry. The two of us looked pretty odd sitting in this empty Chinese restaurant on a night when no one else would dare go out,

with tears running down our faces. I felt I had known
Mike a lot longer than the six months we had been
together.

Washington's Birthday, hospital day, came. I had a
lot of trouble deciding what to take to the hospital. I
had never spent the night in one before and I didn't
know what I would need. In the end I took a few
nightgowns, some socks, and a whole bunch of my
school books. I was determined to keep up with my
reading so that when I returned to college I wouldn't be
behind in my classes. I wasn't going to foul up like I did
last semester. This semester had been going so well.

It seemed to take forever the next morning to get
checked into the hospital. My mother and father went
with me. My father had to fill out lots of papers. Luckily I was still covered under his medical insurance policy. The formalities over, I found myself in room 914,
Albert Einstein College Hospital. To my surprise it was
a private room. I was pleased about that. I didn't really
want to talk to other patients and have to explain why I
was there. I still hadn't completely come to terms with
what was happening and I didn't want to have to cope
with strangers' questions. (Although I thought I got the
private room by chance, I found out later that Dr. Daniel had requested it for me.)

I didn't want to change into a nightgown. It was still
early in the day and I didn't feel sick. Why did they
want me to play sick and get into this bed? I refused to
even sit on the bed; I walked around the room looking
out the windows at the view of the Bronx. Considering
it was the Bronx it was really quite scenic.

My mother helped me put my clothes away, and I
chatted nervously with my parents for a while. Soon a
doctor came in. It wasn't Dr. Daniel but the resident
for that floor. He looked awfully young.

He said he was there to examine me—a pelvic exam.
Now I had to get out of my clothes and into the night-

gown. Nurses and aides started coming in and out. I was weighed, and my temperature and blood pressure were taken. After these preliminaries, I was escorted to a little closet of a room into which an examining table barely squeezed. The resident was going to examine me there. I didn't like this at all, it was so cramped. The doctor tried to make conversation. It turned out that we had gone to the same high school and even had had some of the same teachers. He thought that was great. It only made me more embarrassed.

His exam was not nearly as quick or as painless as Dr. Daniel's had been, but it was soon over and I was allowed to go back to my room again. I was a bit shaken. I hadn't expected them to start the action so fast. After all, it was a holiday. The rest of the day was spent checking out the hospital equipment—how to make the bed go up and down, how to work the TV. Mike came by in the afternoon. We chattered mindlessly. Jokes were made about the food. The time passed too quickly.

The hardest part was when it was time for everyone to go home. Visiting hours started at 11:00 A.M. and ended at 8:30 P.M., but my parents lingered until 9:00, and Mike stayed a little longer to say goodnight. Finally they were all gone and I was alone. Very alone.

My stay in the hospital seemed to be divided into two stages. The first was the testing stage. From the day I entered the hospital I felt that every portion of my body was being poked at, looked at, X-rayed, or biopsied. It was grueling. It was tiring. It was dehumanizing. Each day I was scheduled for two or more tests. Each day brought a new horror. Dr. Daniel and his associate, Dr. Charlton, explained to me that all these tests were necessary to determine my condition—in other words, whether the cancer had spread, and if so, to where.

38

At this point, nobody had mentioned treatment options to me—whether it would be surgery, chemotherapy, or radiology therapy. The doctors were probably as much in the dark as I was. They themselves weren't sure which option would be the best. Meanwhile, they wanted to know everything about my body.

All the testing was a strange experience for me. I had never gone through a battery of physical examinations before; I had always been well. At the hospital I tried to be a "good patient," vague though that term is. I guess I tried not to be difficult, believing the doctors when they said things like, "This won't hurt." I tried to relax and go through the tests without too much complaining. But over and over again, whatever anyone said, there *was* pain and discomfort during every procedure. And I was still so much in the dark; they poked but didn't tell me what they found. I always ended up back in my room, totally exhausted, still frightened and alone. I was maintaining my brave image as much as I could, but if no one was around, the tears would flow.

One of the first tests was the IVP (intravenous pyelogram). For an IVP a lab technician injects dye into the body and this allows X-rays to be taken of the kidneys. Since my lesion was on my cervix and vagina, the doctors explained that they were particularly concerned about my entire urogenital area. So the IVP was important.

Getting prepared for the IVP, I had my first experience with hospital dressing gowns. (They never let me take any tests in my own nightgown.) I could never figure out which was the correct way for these things to go on. Should they be tied in the front or in the back? Whichever way I did it, it was always the wrong way for any particular test. I was constantly humiliated by these wretched gowns, but as time went on it became clear to me that much of a patient's obedience was founded on a loss of dignity.

For the IVP, I think my dressing gown was tied at the back. I lay on the examining table, flat out—I didn't have to have my legs up for a change. "I'm going to inject a dye into you," the lab technician explained. "It will feel warm and it's possible that you will start to feel very hot and even nauseous."

I hadn't gone into this test scared. It was one of the tests my father had had when he had been ill, and he had spent some time discussing it with me before I went for mine. He reassured me that it was painless and explained the whole procedure to me. He had mentioned the warmth but not the feeling of heat or nausea. I had believed my father. I always believed my father. Why was this lab technician scaring me? I had visions of vomiting all over myself, the table, and the X-ray machine. I used to vomit a lot as a kid. Whenever I became nervous I used to vomit. I once embarrassed myself terribly in front of my whole fifth-grade class when we went to the World's Fair in New York. While waiting to go to an exhibit I barfed in front of everyone. I was even more embarrassed when everyone asked if I was sick, because my best friend's mother, who was escorting us, said, "No, she does this all the time."

And now it was going to happen again. I told myself not to panic.

In went the dye. It did feel a little warm, but it wasn't unbearable. No heat, no nausea. Within a few minutes the technician had started to poke the X-ray machine on me. Still no nausea. There was a small TV in the lab that showed what the X-ray would be taking pictures of. The technician pointed it out to me and said I was now looking at my own kidneys. They didn't look much like the kidneys I had studied in textbooks, but I took his word for it. Those were my kidneys. Please be well, kidneys, I prayed. "Right," said the technician. "Inhale and hold. It will be over in a few seconds." I inhaled and held while he went behind a metal screen to operate the machine. I wondered what this radiation was doing to me. Click, click. It was done. This test was over and I hadn't vomited. Dad was right, after all.

The IVP hadn't been too bad, but it would be all downhill from there.

Of all the days of testing, the worst was when I was scheduled for the proctoscopy and the barium enema. That was more than any person should be forced to endure. The day before, the nurse had given me castor oil. I had been totally unprepared for it. The worst part was that it was Sunday, when I had a lot of visitors. Everyone was there—parents, Michael, brother, sister, aunts, uncles, and friends. As always, the nurses were being extremely tolerant (one of the advantages of having a private room) and allowed me to have more than the usual maximum number of two visitors at a time. I was feeling pretty cheerful and optimistic when the nurse came in and said she had to give me medication. Most of my visitors left the room, not wanting to be in the nurse's way, but I asked Mike and my mother to stay behind. The nurse handed me a full medicine cup of what looked like cooking oil, poured me a glass of water, and told me to drink. I knew it wasn't going to go down easily. Mom gave me some encouragement, and I started to swallow. It was disgusting. It just oozed all over my throat. The water didn't do much; it just slid over the castor oil. It certainly didn't help the oil go down. Eventually I managed to swallow it, horrible though it was. When Dad came back, Mom explained to him why I looked as though I had been sucking on lemons, and he said they should have given me orange juice to take with it. That always helps a lot, he said; water does nothing. Thanks, Dad, I thought, where were you a few minutes ago?

That evening I was put on a liquid diet. Of course, once the castor oil started to take effect I didn't have time to eat anything anyway. Then early the next morning the nurse came in carrying a large bedpan with lots of peculiar tubing and a strange smile on her face. Time for the enema.

I hated every second of it. By the time the nurse had finished and I had wiped the tears from my eyes, I just wanted to get into bed and stay there for the rest of the day. But, unfortunately, my day was only just beginning.

I was wheeled downstairs and dropped off in a waiting room. I was going to have the proctoscopy first. This was a test to determine whether the cancer had spread to my colon. I couldn't imagine how they were going to stick anything up my ass—after the effects of the castor oil and enema. I waited there for quite a while, and finally it was my turn.

In the examining room was a tall, middle-aged doctor. He spoke with the most charming British accent. He told me to kneel down on a strange examining table while he adjusted it in such a way that my bare butt was pointing up to the sky. Thank God I couldn't see what he was doing after that. Feeling it was bad enough. It seemed as though this hose was piercing inside me and would never stop. Suddenly his charming accent wasn't so charming anymore, especially since he kept saying, "My dear, relax your arse, relax." I started to faint, so what does the doctor do? He tilts his little table so that my head is down lower and my ass is up higher.

Once that was over I felt like an old rag. I felt used, mangled, intruded upon, and violated. I had no dignity left at all. I wanted to crawl into bed, but it wasn't time yet to go back to the room. I had to have the barium first.

I admit to being very naive about hospital procedures. When the doctors and nurses said I was going to have a barium that day, I pictured myself drinking a glass of milky, chalky substance and then having X-rays taken.

I was sitting in a different waiting room now. There were lots of other patients—inpatients and outpatients —all waiting to be called for their tests. I looked pretty washed out from my last test, and some of the others started talking to me. The main topic of conversation was the barium. And those who had had it before said how horrible it tasted. I told them I had never had it before and was immediately bombarded with helpful hints on how to get the stuff down. Some suggested holding the nose, others suggested swallowing it quickly in big gulps. I was hardly listening to all the advice; I just kept thinking that even though I had got away without vomiting during the IVP, I wasn't going to get away without it here.

This department was really backed up and I was waiting there for an hour and a half. I so wanted to get it over with and go back to my room, and at one point I went up to the nurse at the desk to plead for mercy. She just told me that I had to wait and there was nothing they could do about it. Had I known what was to come I would have gladly just sat and waited there for a *day* before going in that room.

Finally it was my turn. I swallowed hard, getting ready for that glass of barium to arrive. But instead I was ushered into a large X-ray room. A huge bag of white, chalky-looking liquid hung down next to the table in the middle of the room. I stood there for a second with my mouth open in horror. Panic seized me. I wanted to run. This was not the drinking barium, this was the enema barium. Of course, I should have realized they would be interested in my lower tract. I could not believe they were going to shove more things up my ass. My body just couldn't take it. I was still very sore and in pain from the proctoscopy. The nurse took my arm. There was no escape. I was placed on the table and the staff followed their routine. They inserted the enema tube and started to fill me up. I kept taking deep breaths, trying to keep calm, but I couldn't.

DES DAUGHTER

The liquid kept coming. And coming. "That's enough," I moaned weakly. "I can't hold any more." "You have to," the lab technician said, "just a little more."

But it was a lot more. It felt as though my insides were going to burst. I was doing my best to hold it in, but now, instead of worrying about vomiting all over the place, I was afraid I couldn't control my sphincter and would let the barium out. I started to get tears in my eyes. "Please, that's enough. I can't hold it. Please." I pleaded in vain. In fact, my protests began to annoy the lab technician and the nurse. "You must take more, and if you let it out, we'll just have to start over again. You don't want to go through this again, do you?" They tilted the table, with my head down and feet up, at quite an angle. They hoped that gravity would help me. All it did was make me feel that I was going to go sliding off the table head first at any moment.

I suppose it did help because finally the two of them agreed that there was at last enough barium in my body. I asked if they could hurry with the X-rays because I didn't know how long I could hold it in. Unfortunately, that day I had tied the dressing gown in front, so that when the lab technician started poking me with the X-ray machine, my gown undid itself. There I was, completely exposed and tilted upside down, with a man pressing down on my intestines with a heavy machine while I was trying not to let out the barium. It was my picture of hell.

Once it was over, I was able to cover up and go to the bathroom that was just off the examining room. Even that was painful, although a relief.

Back in the waiting room, I had to wait for an orderly to wheel me back up to my room. They wouldn't let me go by myself. I tried to be patient because at least everything for that day was over, but it took an hour for someone to come. I was exasperated; it was the last straw. I felt washed out and totally dehumanized that day. I was powerless, there was no control left. Why was this happening?

Back at my room, my mother was waiting for me. It was after 3:00 P.M. My lunch was there waiting for me, ice cold. Even though I hadn't eaten since the night before, I had only enough energy to climb into bed and fall asleep.

The next day's test was the cystoscopy. This one didn't scare me as much. At least I was somewhat familiar with it, since it had been talked about in my house quite a bit. My father had cystoscopy done to him every six months or so. He had to have his bladder checked regularly because he had a tendency to develop tumors in this area. Dad always said that the cystoscopy was nothing, and now, when I was to have one performed, he reassured me. "Don't worry, it doesn't hurt. You just feel a little pressure. And besides, you're a girl. It's worse for a man."

It is worse for a man because in this test a tubelike instrument, the cystoscope, is inserted up through the urinary tract right into the bladder. This enables the doctor to see into that area of the body and detect any abnormalities or growths.

I didn't have to wait very long, for a change, and before I knew it, I was on my back on a table with my rear end placed over an opening. A technician, wearing a surgical gown and mask, poured an orange-colored disinfectant on me from my navel to the top of my thighs. It was a startling and uncomfortable feeling, almost like urinating in bed. I felt embarrassed—and I looked orange.

The physician came in and introduced himself as Dr. Tein. He was a short, stocky, middle-aged man with a baby face. I didn't take much notice of him. I was feeling very sorry for myself and was very tense. The doctor stuck something in my arm. I couldn't make out exactly what it was, but liquid was dripping into my veins. I think it was to calm me down. Dr. Tein then looked at my urinary opening and started inserting the tube, very slowly and carefully. Dad was right; it doesn't hurt but it is uncomfortable, and you certainly know it's there. I felt so helpless and pathetic lying there, I couldn't control myself and started to cry. I felt so broken and weak. My sobs were no longer rebellious and loud; they were more like sad, depressed whimpers. Dr. Tein noticed what was happening and came over to me. He didn't say anything, he just took my hand and held on to it for a few minutes. He really did care, and it showed on his face. He went back to the procedure and tried so hard to be gentle and quick. I will always remember him for that.

When it was over, I was put on a gurney to go back to my room. In the elevator, I looked around me and noticed the person standing next to the gurney. She was a woman I knew from high school. She saw me and looked startled. We didn't say a word to each other and when the elevator reached the ninth floor I was wheeled off, leaving her behind.

The next day I received an orchid from Dr. Tein.

After most of the initial testing had been done, Dr. Daniel called for a consultation because there was still no decision made about the method of treatment. I envisioned a consultation among doctors as taking place in a large room around a conference table, with X-rays and reports all around the walls. Unfortunately, in my case anyway, it was nothing like that. The consulting physicians all came together to examine my genitals one by one, in front of each other. I could hardly believe it when they all trooped into the examining room.

I have always been a very shy person. (I didn't speak to anyone outside of my immediate family until I was nine years old.) Having to put up with the testing so far had been hard enough and I certainly didn't relish the thought of having all these men focusing their attention on my body. Perhaps with the right wine, sexy negligee, and soft lights it could have been the setting for a kinky sexual encounter, but the way this scene played itself I felt like a super-freak on display for all to come and see.

Thank God for the nurses. The one present on this occasion was perceptive enough to realize that I might feel a little uncomfortable in the circumstances. She tried to spend the minimal amount of time assisting the physicians and most of her time standing next to me holding my hand. It may seem like an insignificant gesture, but for the one on the receiving end, having something real to grasp and a face to look into offered great comfort.

While I was holding the nurse's hand, a line was forming at the other end of my body. It consisted of Dr. Daniel, Dr. Charlton, an anesthesiologist, a radiologist, a chemotherapist, and a surgeon. Six doctors, all to see me. Somehow I didn't feel very lucky.

I was told to sit up while they looked me over. One of the doctors made a comment about my skin. I had been troubled by a moderate case of acne since the age of fourteen. It wasn't very serious and I had always expected it to clear up by itself. This doctor looked at my face and said, "Have you ever seen a doctor about your acne?"

"No," I squeaked out. I was astonished by the question.

"Haven't you been concerned about the condition of your complexion at *your* age?"

I was only eighteen years old! The way the doctor said this made me feel guilty, as if zits were an early warning sign for cancer! At least for the moment my own attention was drawn up from my vagina to my face. Suddenly, sitting there naked in front of six middle-aged men, I was embarrassed by the way my face looked.

On my back again. It was impossible for all six doctors to get a good view of my vagina and cervix at the same time, so they lined up. Thank goodness there was no arguing about who should go first. Each man would peer between my thighs and take a good long look while Dr. Daniel or Dr. Charlton pointed out the areas of interest. The other specialists made their own comments and observations as they went along. None of this was directed to me. The only words spoken to me were things like, "Could you spread your legs a little wider, please," or "You're doing just fine, this will be over in a minute."

During all this, the nurse kept squeezing my hand. She herself was young, with brown eyes, dark hair, and a pretty smile. I can't remember what any of the doctors looked like, apart from Dr. Daniel and Dr. Charlton, of course, but I will always remember what that nurse looked like.

After about half an hour, the doctors thanked me for being such a remarkable patient and left. I put on my nightgown and waited in the hall for my escort back to my room. While I sat there, I suddenly saw Dr. Levinstein, our family doctor. He was our doctor long before I was even born. He was the one who had taken care of me whenever I had a cold, the measles, chicken pox, and all those childhood illnesses. He was also the one who referred my mother to the obstetrician, Dr. Fleischer, who supervised her pregnancy with me and gave her the DES. Dr. Levinstien had been called in by Dr. Daniel to join the doctors' consultation meeting about me, which was about to start. He spent a few moments talking to me, though he didn't say much and did not specifically discuss my cancer. I felt a strong urge to ask him if he thought my acne was really that

bad, but I thought better of it and kept quiet. Within a
few minutes he too was gone.

Of all the tests I was having, the one I knew least
about before was the D & C. I didn't really know what
it was, but it seemed that a lot of women had had it. Of
course, these women were older than I, but from what I
could gather, there didn't seem to be any great risk
involved. I discovered that D & C stood for dilation and
curettage. My cervix would be dilated and the sides
of my uterus scraped, thus enabling the doctors to see
what condition the inside of my uterus was in. The
most frightening part was that it is done as a surgical
procedure, under general anesthesia.

The day before my D & C I was "prepped" for it.
This consisted of a nurse shaving off all the hair from
my midsection to the middle of my thighs. It seemed
like an awfully large area! I felt like a plucked chicken.
That evening I was put on a liquid diet and couldn't eat
or drink anything after midnight.

The next morning I was up early and ready to be
taken down to the operating room. The nurse had
brought in the hospital gown that I had to put on before
being taken down there. I felt a little chilly while waiting for the orderly to come and collect me, so I put on a
pair of socks to keep my feet warm. The socks happened to belong to Mike. Somehow they were amongst
the few clothes I had brought with me to the hospital. I
realized this when I pulled them on and saw how they
hung off my feet. My feet are not small but they are not
as large as Mike's. The socks looked so odd as to be
comforting, and I felt good that they were Mike's.

In came the orderly. I hopped onto the gurney and
stuck my feet under the sheets. I was wheeled off for
my D & C.

I was parked right outside the inner doors where the
surgery rooms were. I began to feel rather nervous and

shaky. I seemed to be in the waiting area, because there were other people around on their gurneys. The time passed slowly. I felt apprehensive. A nurse appeared and put a cap on the top of my head to cover my hair. "Are you starting to feel relaxed?" she asked.

"Not at all," I replied, startled. "Why should I?"

"Haven't you had a Demerol injection to help you calm down?"

"No," I said.

"You should have had one in your room, before coming down here." She sounded concerned and went off to find some Demerol. I was glad that I was going to get something to calm my nerves.

To my horror, I was suddenly pushed into the operating room before the nurse had returned. I was placed on a table, my legs up in stirrups once again. Dr. Daniel was there with a few people I didn't recognize. Someone remarked in horrified tones that I had socks on. He was obviously shocked to see my absurd-looking, unsterile socks when everyone was wearing their clean white surgical gear. Once again, I was embarrassed. Dr. Daniel responded quickly and said it was all right for me to keep the socks on. I appreciated that.

The anesthesiologist arrived and she realized immediately that I hadn't had any Demerol to calm me down. (I was shaking so much.) She rapidly hooked up her equipment to put me under. Standing behind me, over my head, she looked down at me and asked, "Have you ever had a martini?"

I thought it was a very peculiar question to ask at this time. "No," I said. (I still drank only sangria and those other, less sophisticated beverages.)

"Well," she said, "once I start this sodium pentothal it will feel like ten martinis!" Seconds later she asked me to start counting backward from one hundred. By the time I got to 98 I was fast asleep.

Before my eyes opened I could hear the soft voices of my mother and my Aunt Ruthy talking back and forth. I could feel the warmth and brightness of the sun shining into the room. I felt groggy and dry in my mouth and when I opened my eyes, Mom was there to give me a big hello. She swabbed my mouth with a moistened Q-tip as I slowly felt myself falling back to sleep. Before I did, I rubbed my feet together and realized that I still had my socks on.

CHAPTER 4

My fear that Dr. Daniel would not be honest with me about my condition was totally unfounded. I really grew to love this man. As hard as his outside appearance was, inside he was caring and sensitive. He certainly was not perfect—all too often I felt as though I were being treated like a collection of malignant cells, rather than as a person—but in general he was frank about my condition and, more importantly, he did not treat me like a child.

I made it clear from the beginning that honesty was important. I was so afraid that I would not be told the truth. I kept thinking that there was a real possibility that I was dying, and if I were, I wanted to know. I *had* to know, because I didn't want to spend my last days worrying about my schoolwork and about how much I was missing. At least while I was in the hospital, my thoughts never went beyond that concern.

Dr. Daniels always told me why tests were being done, though he never said what would happen if the results came back positive. But then I never asked him. In fact, as time went on, I did less and less asking in the hospital. I knew that soon enough they would be coming in with my verdict, and I already had a pretty good idea of what it would be. I felt that surgery was imminent and only feared that the treatment wouldn't be enough.

I could tell that Dr. Daniel liked me. He'd come by my room whenever he was in the hospital and would usually find me, after a day of exhausting tests, with several visitors. Mike was almost always there, lying next to me in the hospital bed. It was great and special.

52

I would lie there in nightgown and robe, with the head section of the bed raised up to nearly a sitting position, and Mike would be next to me—fully clothed, of course. It was our only way of having real contact with each other, and it gave everyone else a laugh. More important, it made me feel less isolated as a sick person. So many people wouldn't come close to me because I was "sick," as though they were afraid of catching something from me. You lose a lot of body contact with people when you're in the hospital. But Mike didn't let that happen. In fact, he couldn't keep his hands off me—nor I mine off him. I think my being in nightgowns all the time really turned us on.

Whenever Dr. Daniel came in to see the two of us like this, I had the feeling that though he growled about this behavior on the outside, he was actually laughing about it on the inside. He knew it made me happy, and that's what he was concerned about just then. Whenever Mike wasn't around, he always made a point of asking where he was.

Today was the day when Dr. Daniel was going to tell me the verdict. All the tests had been done, and he was going to let me· know exactly where I stood and what the treatment plan would be.

I was nervous. Deep inside I sensed that surgery was coming. The week before I had finally managed to talk to Mike about it. I had been wondering how he would feel if I had to have a hysterectomy. How important were children to him? We had spoken of our love for each other so often recently. We hadn't committed ourselves to marriage—we both felt too young for that— yet we realized that our relationship had depth and feeling, and we sensed it would be long lasting. But all the same, I didn't know if Mike would change his mind if he knew there would never be any possibility of my having children. After all there was nothing to hold him to me. Yet the thought of his leaving was so painful. Right then, he was what gave me the reason, the energy, the courage to tolerate each day of my ordeal. The pain, the frustration, the anger all melted away every time he walked into my room. This beautiful man loved me even though I had cancer. But would he love me even though I could never bear children? I knew I had to talk to him about it.

My parents were very understanding and often went for "strolls" around the hospital to allow Mike and me to spend some time alone together.

"When will you know what they'll do to you?" Mike asked as he lay beside me.

"Dr. Daniel's going to talk to me next week, once he has the results from all the tests. I hope he tells me the truth."

"I'm sure he will. And if he doesn't, I'll make sure I find out from your parents what he tells them. You can be sure that I'll tell you about it right away."

"Do you promise?"

"Honest, I promise I'll tell you everything. You know I will, I love you."

"I know."

Mike paused. "It'll probably be a hysterectomy, you know." He had obviously been thinking about this too.

"Yeah, that's what I figure it will have to be. I only hope that they can get it all with the surgery. If they tell me that I have to have chemotherapy, I'll know it's all over."

"That's not necessarily true. Now don't worry about that until you hear what they have to say." He hugged me close.

"I'm trying not to. I'm scared about the hysterectomy. I don't want them to do that either."

"If it helps you," Mike said softly, "that's all that counts."

"But I won't be able to have children." I looked at him squarely.

"But you'll be okay. And I'll still love you whether or not you can have kids."

I was fighting back tears. "Will you? Will you really?" He was saying everything I wanted to hear. I could hardly believe it.

"Sure," Mike went on. "I have never told you this before but one of my great fears in life is that I'll have a kid and it'll be the ugliest child in the world. I wouldn't want to take the risk. If you can't have kids, it just means there's one less thing in this world for me to worry about."

Laughing and crying, I held onto him tightly and managed to tell him that I loved him.

After my talk with Mike, I was prepared to hear what the doctors had decided to do for me, or to me.

Early that morning Mom and Dad came to see me. Mom was wearing sunglasses so I knew she had been crying and didn't want me to see that. I could tell that they had already been told the verdict; they were trying too hard to be cheerful. My mother kept patting me on the head, and they weren't really talking to me properly. We didn't say much, and I didn't want to hear anything. I suddenly felt that I wasn't ready; I didn't want to know.

"The doctors are waiting outside now," Mom said. "They want to come in and talk to you. Do you want us to stay?"

I knew the news wasn't good, and I couldn't stand to be told it with my parents watching. I already felt like crying but was still acting brave and holding back the tears so as not to upset them.

"No," I said. "I'd rather talk to them alone."

"Fine," said my mother. Both she and Dad kissed me before leaving the room. I thought they looked a little hurt.

Within minutes Dr. Daniel came in, followed by Dr. Romney, the chief of the gynecology department at Albert Einstein College Hospital. Dr. Romney had come to see me before. A short, stocky man, he came across as rather cold and hard.

I sat up, and the doctors sat themselves in chairs at the foot of the bed.

"Now, Joyce," said Dr. Daniel, "would you mind if some OB-GYN residents and interns are present while Dr. Romney and I talk to you?"

"It would be a good learning experience for them, but it is entirely up to you, of course," said Dr. Romney.

I had an image of a long line of people waiting outside my room for admittance to the side show. Step right up and watch her cry!

Learning experience or not, I did not want to be gawked at. "No," I said firmly. They went on.

Dr. Daniel explained that the test results were all back and that everyone had gone over them very carefully, so that they were confident about their decision.

"Uh-huh." I was waiting. My hands were twisting the sheets.

"A great deal of sexuality is in the head," Dr. Daniel said. "People can have orgasms just by imagining certain things. It's all very much psychological. . . . All in the mind. . . ."

I couldn't believe that I was hearing this. What are they trying to tell me? I thought. What are they going to cut out? He's telling me I can't have an orgasm except in my head? I felt a jolt as I realized what was really being said. My God, I thought, I was only thinking about my uterus, but my external genitalia too? (I suddenly remembered all I had learned in a sexuality course during my first semester at college. I knew that the most sensitive area and the key to orgasm was located externally). Tears were pouring down my face. "You're going to remove my clitoris?" I almost shouted. I was too horrified to care about being a "good" patient anymore.

Both doctors looked taken aback. "No, no," they said in unison.

"Then why are you talking to me about orgasms?" I demanded.

"Well," said Dr. Romney, surprisingly gently, "because we will have to do a hysterectomy . . . and we will have to remove your vagina."

My heart thumped in my chest. I yelled, "My vagina? How do you remove a vagina? You're not talking about not having an orgasm; how can you have sex at all without a vagina?"

I broke down completely. How could the news be so bad? The doctors kept talking but I could only catch bits and pieces through my uncontrollable sobbing.

". . . We won't touch anything external. Your clitoris will have total sensation. . . . After this operation, at a later time, you can have reconstructive surgery. . . . We plan on leaving you with an ovary. . . . You will have hormones. . . ."

They went on and on. I missed a lot of it. Finally, Dr. Daniel asked how I thought Michael would feel about all this. I pulled myself together enough to answer. I stopped sobbing, though the tears never stopped coming down. I told them that Michael and I had already discussed the likelihood of a hysterectomy and that it didn't matter to him as long as it would help me.

"You mean you've both talked about a hysterectomy already?" asked Dr. Daniel.

"Yes," I said, suddenly feeling calm. "We thought that it would be probable, considering my problems." I couldn't believe how I was able to answer so dispassionately. I wasn't feeling very much by now; I felt more like a stone wall than a human being.

"Well," said Dr. Daniel, looking very relieved. "Here Dr. Romney and I were, concerned about how to tell you about this and you have already discussed it. You're amazing."

"We never talked about my vagina, though," I said

coldly. I was finding it hard talking about orgasms and vaginas to these fatherly-looking men. Was I glad the entire resident staff wasn't in there with us.

"As we said," Dr. Daniel replied, "that can be reconstructed in a separate surgical procedure."

"Will I be able to . . . you know . . . have sex?"

"Absolutely." Both the doctors were obviously trying to sound cheerful, but they looked fairly awkward as they took their leave and left the room.

My parents came back in immediately. I wasn't really crying anymore. I was just trying to let everything sink in. I told Mom and Dad that everything would be all right, that I had been prepared for it.

They didn't mention the vaginectomy. They were just there, and that alone was a tremendous comfort. I could only imagine what Mom was thinking. How it must hurt her, I thought, to know that a drug that she had taken so innocently when she was pregnant was now causing her daughter to have her uterus and vagina removed. I didn't want my mother to hurt. I didn't want her to feel guilty. We hadn't spoken any more about DES since the telephone conversation with Dr. Daniel, but we both were aware of the connection between the drug and my cancer. I told her that I loved her. I didn't want her to see my pain; I had to be brave.

I could see the pain in my father's face. I was his little girl, and his little girl was hurt. It was as if he were experiencing my pain for me. I knew I had to be brave for him, too. I realized then how very much I loved them both.

Soon they left the room. I think they sensed that I needed a chance to be alone. I called Michael up at work. He was still working at the small clothing store in Manhattan and going to school at night. It had been difficult for him because of all of the time he spent with me in the hospital. But he managed not to lose his job and seemed to be doing all right in school. By the time

I got through to him my wall of bravery had pretty much collapsed and I could barely get the words out. Yes, it would be a hysterectomy. We expected that. "But," I blurted out, "they're also going to remove my vagina!" I was crying so hard it was difficult to say the words. I don't know what I expected Mike to do or say. I was afraid he would be disgusted and repulsed—and who could blame him? It was hard to imagine how a vagina can be removed, let alone what life would be like without one.

Mike was shocked. He didn't say much. Mainly he listened or tried to calm me down. I told him I needed him and asked if he could come right over. He said he'd be there.

When he arrived, he stood by the door for a second or two and we just stared at each other. Then I threw myself into his arms and hung on to him. Mike held me tight and rocked me back and forth as if I were seven years old. It felt good. I needed the comforting from him.

I told him again that they were going to remove my vagina. I don't think I really believed he had heard me the first time, and I don't think I really believed it yet. I had to say it over, to hear the words. But when I did, I felt even more appalled at the thought. It was so mutilating, so freakish. Whoever heard of such a thing? It wasn't something that you hear about; it was unnatural and it was bizarre and they were going to do it to *me*. "It doesn't matter, Joyce," Mike finally said. "I still love you, and I'm only glad that the doctors can help you. You're going to be okay, that's the main thing."

I watched Mike closely as he said all this. I had to see if he was able to look at me properly—in the eye. Was he saying this, I wondered, just to make me feel better? Would he later walk out the door so I'd never see him again? But he did seem sincere. I wanted to think I could be brave enough to handle this without him, but he was so comforting, so good, and I was so much in love, I wanted him to be there. I started to become afraid that he wouldn't be.

Later that day, when visiting hours were over and Mike and my parents had gone home, I was alone. I was alone and I was afraid. I didn't want to be on my own. I didn't want to think about the surgery and what was going to be done to me in a few short days. I fell into my pillow and wept bitterly. Within a few minutes, Diane, one of the nurses on the floor walked in. During my two weeks in the hospital, I had come to like her a lot. She was young, pleasant, friendly, and always seemed so secure and competent. She had sensed I needed someone and she was there. She didn't come in to give me medications, or to take my temperature or my blood pressure. Diane was there just to be there. I cried to her about how unfair it was that I had to lose my uterus and vagina, and she just held me. I cried to her that I was afraid and that I wished it wasn't happening to me. She made sure I had enough tissues to cry into.

I don't know how she managed to spare the time, but Diane spent over an hour with me until I was so worn out I couldn't cry anymore. And I didn't cry anymore. I suddenly felt stronger and able to handle what was coming. At least now I knew what to expect. The monster had an image—it was an image of cancer and of surgery, but I was determined to survive. I had finished crying for now.

CHAPTER 5

Two days before my surgery was scheduled I was visited by a tall, young woman who introduced herself as the hospital social worker. I noticed that she was wearing a woolen vest that was just like the one I had bought for myself right before my hospitalization. I mentioned this to her and we laughed. I wanted to talk about the vest; I didn't want to give her a chance to talk to me about my imminent surgery. But there's not all that much that can be said about a vest, and soon we were talking about the surgery.

She wanted to know about my relationship with Michael. She seemed concerned that we had known each other for so short a period of time. I got the feeling that she was preparing me for the fact that he might not be around for me to lean on. That annoyed me, probably because she was forcing me to confront my worst fears. Yet she impressed me. She impressed me because she was someone to whom I had no emotional ties, neither a relative nor a friend, yet she took the time to listen to me and she cared enough to talk about the things that most strangers would feel too uncomfortable to talk to me about.

She didn't stay long, but after she had gone I felt better. It had been helpful to talk to her. I still didn't like the idea that I had to go through with the surgery, but it was going to happen and I was starting to accept that fact.

The day before the surgery Mike came to visit me. My father was at work and my mother hadn't arrived, so we were alone together again. The nurses on the floor were all busy elsewhere, and the door to my room was closed.

We talked about things to come and how much we loved each other. I felt that after the next day, my body would be terribly damaged and I had no idea if I'd have any sensations left afterward. I suppose I just wanted to use the equipment I had while I still had it.

Time was growing short. We started kissing and hugging and touching. We went into the bathroom so that if a nurse walked in we wouldn't be caught surprised. We couldn't actually do very much, simply because I was scheduled for surgery the next day and we were afraid of doing some damage. But it was enough, and we enjoyed each other's intimate embraces, knowing that it would never be exactly like this again. I treasured those moments because I knew that even if they could reconstruct what they had removed, it would never be the same.

Later that day, Dr. Daniel and Dr. Charlton came by to talk to me. They wanted to tell me what to expect and to answer my questions. I appreciated this meeting, not only because they were being honest with me but also because an air of confidence emanated from them, and I sensed it. However, they did tell me some disturbing things. Although all the X-rays and tests had come back negative, which meant that they could not detect the presence of cancer in any organs other than my cervix and vagina, it appeared that some of my organs were pushed up against each other, so that the doctors weren't sure they had gotten a total picture from the X-rays. Because of this, they said they would have to explore my organs carefully during the surgery, and they couldn't tell me exactly what condition I would find myself in when I woke up from surgery.

Dr. Daniel could tell me that they would be removing my uterus, they would be removing one ovary, they would be removing my vagina. I would have several tubes in me when I woke up. One in my bladder, one in my arm, one from my wound, and possibly, he said, one down my nose into my stomach. I asked about this one—it disturbed me. He explained that since the X-rays were not clear, they would have to examine my stomach carefully and if they had to touch my stomach too much, then they would need to put tubes into it so that I would not have a problem with vomiting immediately after the surgery. I didn't like hearing this at all. What Dr. Daniel was trying to tell me was that there was still a real possibility that the cancer had spread. I knew that but didn't want to think about it. I focused my fear on the tube, imagining how uncomfortable it would be to have a tube running down my nose and throat into my stomach.

When the doctors left, I kept thinking that I could handle the hysterectomy and vaginectomy but I only hoped that they wouldn't have to put in the tube.

That night I received many telephone calls from friends and relatives all trying to cheer me up and keep me busy. Rosey, Marlene, and my other dormmates sent me a stuffed animal that became a constant source of comfort. Arlene and Bob brought over this huge stuffed purple sheepdog that made me laugh. One call came late in the evening, after visiting hours when everyone had already gone home. This call was from one of my friends' mothers. She is a middle-aged woman with several children of her own. I knew her fairly well, since I had spent a lot of time in her house visiting with my friend. She called to try to give me some comfort and to help me feel better, but I could tell from the sound of her voice that it was she who was horrified at what I was having to go through.

"You know, Joyce," she said, "once you go into surgery, the doctors will probably see that you don't need a hysterectomy after all. I shouldn't worry, if I were you."

"It's definite," I replied firmly. I was annoyed that she seemed to be trying to convince herself that everything was really okay.

"You never know," she went on, "once they can look inside you, you'll see, they won't have to do it."

Something snapped. I raised my voice. "Yes! Yes they *will* do it!" I started screaming into the phone. "I want them to do it! I want them to do it! It will make me well." I was shaking with rage.

My caller was evidently shocked by my reaction—she had, after all, thought she was helping. But I just hung up on her. I didn't know what else to do. I was quite shocked and stunned that I had responded like that. It was then I realized for the first time that my greatest fear was not that I would wake up without a uterus or a vagina, and not be able to make babies, but that the doctors wouldn't be able to help me, that they wouldn't be able to take out all the horrible cancer in me, and that I would die. Let them sacrifice some organs so long as I would live. I wanted to survive. My biggest fear was that I would not.

The next morning I was up at 5:00 A.M. It was still dark out. A nurse came in and prepared me for surgery, mainly by giving me an enema. By 6:00 A.M. my parents had arrived. They looked very worried but were putting on brave faces. Mike wasn't coming by. I think he thought that the tension of waiting around all day would be too much for him. Soon, the nurse came in again and gave me a welcome shot of Demerol. Unfortunately, that stuff doesn't knock you out, but it does do wonders to calm you.

By 7:30 A.M. I was ready to go. I hugged and kissed Mom and Dad and climbed onto the gurney. It will all be over soon, I kept thinking, as I was wheeled down to the operating room. Obviously I felt anxious, but in general I had a sense of resolve. It was real; it was happening. At least it would be over.

In the operating room, I looked up and saw the bright lights glaring down on me. Straight ahead on the wall were two sets of clocks. I thought, Gee, that's just like those television medical shows, when they focus on the clocks to show the passage of time. Meanwhile I was being strapped down to the operating table. My arm was tied down and the anesthesiologist was getting his equipment ready. He stuck something into my arm. Within a few seconds the sodium pentothal was started. Once again I was totally unconscious.

I couldn't open my eyes, but I could hear voices speaking softly behind me. They were saying that it was almost time for another dose of morphine. They were talking about doses and timings. I knew they were talking about me. I thought clearly to myself, I am alive! That was good. I suddenly remembered the tubes. I tried to move my hand up to my face and feel if there were any tubes coming out of my nose, but my arm wouldn't respond at all. I could not lift it up. I swallowed hard. I couldn't feel anything. If the tubes were there, it was okay, because they didn't hurt. I couldn't even feel them. Suddenly I was back asleep.

Pain. Terrible pain, centered in my abdomen but spreading out to all parts of my body. My eyes opened and I looked out through the bars raised around my bed. I couldn't lift my head. Through the bars I could only see people's torsos. I heard the voices of my mother and Michael. I moaned. I wanted them to help me. I heard them run to get the nurse. I heard the nurse, Diane, explaining that I couldn't yet have another pain injection; it was too soon after the last one. But my body hurt, it hurt so much.

When the time did come for the next morphine shot, the sting of the injection felt like a relief compared to the overall agony that I was feeling. I drifted in and out of consciousness throughout the evening of Wednesday,

March 8, 1972, the day my reproductive organs were removed. I had survived that day. Thursday is lost to me. I remember nothing until Friday.

Friday was definitely the start of recovery. I woke up to a new face—Mary. She was the private nurse my parents had arranged for me to have. Mary was smiling as she introduced herself. She was wonderful. A large, strong woman who seemed to be very experienced. She checked my intravenous tubes to make sure they were flowing correctly. The IV was dripping into the top of my left hand. The needle was taped down, but it still made me feel uncomfortable. I made every effort not to move my left arm for fear of poking the needle further into the vein. There was also a catheter running from my bladder to a bag hanging on the side of my bed. Every now and then urine would flow into it. But there were no tubes coming out of my nose. They didn't have to do anything to my stomach. That was a good sign. I felt weak and sore but glad that the surgery was over. Mary told me about all the tubes and what they did. She was positive and enthusiastic—just what I needed at that point.

I learned from my doctors that they had examined all the surrounding organs quite carefully and had found no evidence that the cancer had spread. They had removed the uterus, vagina, one ovary, a bunch of lymph nodes, and my appendix (they said they didn't want me coming back for an appendectomy in the near future). The report was good. I was going to make it. I couldn't help thinking how barbaric the state of medicine still is if the only way to treat this cancer effectively is to cut it out. Just like that. But I was thankful that even though the treatment was unsophisticated, it looked as if it would work—would keep me alive.

Many people came to visit me after the surgery. The regulars were all there—Mom and Dad, Mike, my brother, sister, Mike's parents (who had been wonderful supports throughout this experience)—and many other family members and friends. My room was more like Grand Central Station than a room in a hospital. I learned a lot about friendship during this time. There were some people who were just there whenever you needed them, to talk, bring comfort, and listen. For instance, one friend, Barbara, loaned me her favorite stuffed animal, a hippo, just so I'd have something close and personal nearby for those hours when I was alone. Then there were the others, people I had thought were good friends, who for a variety of reasons, just didn't know how to deal with someone who was sick. These were the people who stayed away from the hospital, who never even called, because they "Didn't know what to say to someone who had cancer." These people are no longer my friends.

Then there was Mike. Mike was supportive, encouraging, and *real*. There was a consistency about the way he treated me before and after my operation that was refreshing. He respected me, didn't baby me, and his attitude toward me gave me strength and courage.

Two days after the operation I got up and started walking. At least I *tried* to walk then. Mary was there to encourage me as I slowly swung my legs over the side of the bed. I felt like an old lady. I could only move in slow motion, and even that was no easy mechanical feat either. I didn't only have to worry about moving my body, but there was all that fancy equipment as well. The IV bottle on the pole had to be wheeled along beside me, and I also had to carry my urine bag wherever I went. Quite a spectacle, and not quite the height of fashion either.

After about half an hour I was able to stand up for a few moments, and managed to get to a chair in my room. What a sense of accomplishment. The only crisis I had was when I first stood up. The change in pressure caused the flow of my IV tube to reverse, so that blood started to back up into the tube. It was an insignificant occurrence, but seeing my blood like that made me stop in my tracks, paralyzed. Mary laughed. I changed my arm position and on we went.

Every time my bandages were changed, I looked away. I just wasn't ready to see the incision. But after about a week's time, I had no choice but to look down. What a sight! There was a six-inch vertical scar running from just under my navel down to an inch below what had been my pubic hairline (again, I had been shaved for the surgery). The stitches were still in. They were shocking to look at, these severe black lines running horizontally across the length of a bright red scar. It reminded me of something out of *The Bride of Frankenstein*. I was going to have to get used to it.

The next two weeks I spent slowly gaining strength. Each day I walked a little farther and ate a little more (I had lost quite a bit of weight throughout this ordeal). The hospital had a pleasant sunroom, where I spent many hours. I would sit there and talk to the other patients. Once the IV had been removed I only had to carry my urine bag around with me. Whenever I sat down, I had to try to hide it under my bathrobe. It was just embarrassing to be talking to someone and then have a stream of yellow liquid suddenly course down into the bag. Very tacky!

During this time I received so much attention from everyone—hospital staff as well as family and friends. My room was always filled with people, flowers, and gifts. And by the time I was ready to leave, the entire room was covered with get-well cards. In a strange way it was wonderful. Everyone told me over and over again what a good patient I was, and how well I handled everything, and how strong I was. I started to believe them. They gave me strength. I had little time to dwell on what had happened. It was over, and I was going to be all right. Now I could just concentrate on getting stronger again. I was looking forward to going home.

In all respects but one I was ready to leave the hospital. The only thing that was preventing it now was the catheter. Dr. Daniel removed it. It was a simple procedure to take it out, but not so simple for me to urinate on my own. After the tube had been removed, I drank glass after glass of liquid during the hours following and spent a lot of time in the bathroom. Nothing happened. Absolutely nothing. I just couldn't feel any pressure in my bladder. By the next morning it was obvious that my bladder wasn't ready to work on its own just yet and that I would have to have the catheter reinserted.

It is a lot easier to take one of those things out than to put it back in. As with the cystoscopy, the sensation is not exactly painful but it is uncomfortable. The nurses kept assuring me that it was a lot easier for a woman than a man. No doubt, I thought, and I didn't complain. But I did think that had I been a man, I wouldn't have been there in the first place.

After a few more days we tried again. Out came the catheter, in went the fluids. Again nothing happened. I was getting discouraged. I had visions of never being able to urinate on my own again. Dr. Charlton came by this time and told me that the reason my bladder wasn't working was that during the operation they had picked it up to examine it and had accidentally dropped it on the floor. He was only kidding, of course.

After three or four reinsertions of the catheter, Dr. Daniel suggested that I go home with it in and then they would try to remove it in a week or so. I didn't like the idea of leaving the hospital with this extra piece of equipment (was it supposed to be compensation for what they had removed?), but I certainly was anxious to go home. It was settled that I would be going home in two days, no matter what.

The next day the catheter was removed just one more time. To my joy my bladder was working. After not having urinated on my own for more than two weeks, it was a strange sensation, though in fact there was almost no sensation at all. There was no feeling of pressure or squeezing from my baldder. It was as though it no longer existed. The flow of urine came out of its own free will; I had very little to do with it. I was to learn that the numbness of my bladder would be something that would never really go away; I would have to learn to remember when to go to the bathroom. With no feeling in my bladder, I no longer had an effective warning system.

But tomorrow I could go home.

CHAPTER 6

It was so good to be home. Mom and Dad had put a lot of "Welcome Home" signs all around the apartment; everything looked clean and fresh. It was great to be back in my own bed again, in my own room. I was still quite sore and had difficulty moving, and I still felt like an old lady. But it was good to be an old lady in my own place.

One striking difference between being home and in the hospital was that at home I suddenly felt less protected. My body hurt still and people were there to help me, but I became afraid that something bad might happen, like tripping over a chair or having someone bump into me. My little nephews and niece came by quite often, and although I loved to see them, I was terrified that they would accidentally run into me because they spent a lot of time running around the apartment. I began walking around with my hands protecting my abdominal area. I couldn't stand any more pain.

I began to get used to looking at my scar although I still felt a bit of a jolt every time I did. The stitches had now been removed, but the scar line still looked very raw and red. I got into the habit of showing it to anyone who was willing to look at it, and even some who weren't so willing. I always watched their reactions very carefully—most people grimaced and turned away. I guess I needed confirmation that it wasn't really so horrible and that people would still care for me even though this had happened. I suppose it was a sick thing to do, but that scar represented everything I had recently gone through. I needed people to accept me and my scar. Also, I was perhaps trying to grab all the attention. I had become used to being the center of things while in the hospital. Being home was different in that regard. Certainly my parents gave me lots of attention, but it wasn't the same as having an entire hospital staff coming in and out of your room all day. Things were much quieter. Recuperating was going to be boring.

Soon the reality of my situation really hit me. I had a lot of time to think. As my body healed, my mind no longer had to focus solely on the physical pain I had endured over the last few weeks. The unique experience of hospital life was over. I was expected to resume the course of my life. But things were different, very different. I knew I was going to survive, but I was going to have to survive without a uterus or a vagina. At this time, it started to sink in that had it not been for the DES, I would still have those organs in my body right now.

I spent the entire spring recuperating. I had accepted the fact that I wasn't going to return to college until September, so I had a long time ahead of me. During these early months, I spent a lot of time in my room with Mike. Mike was there with me as before. He was his old self—laughing, joking, hugging, and kissing me. But it wasn't like before. How could it be? I felt antagonistic toward him. If he laughed, I became angry at him. If he said I looked pretty, I got annoyed. I became a real crab. I refused to trust anything he said, and contradicted him constantly. It got to the point where if Mike said something was black, I would insist it was white. And the most frustrating aspect of all this was that he would almost never argue back. "Okay, have it your way," he would say. That infuriated me. I didn't want to be patronized. I was tired of being consoled and pitied by everyone around me and just couldn't stand a patronizing attitude from Mike, of all people. I wanted a good fight! But he wouldn't fight; he just kept attributing my grouchiness to the fact that I was confined to my room for most of the day.

As time went on, things got worse. I was pretty testy with everyone, but Mike bore the brunt of it. He'd show up every evening after work and after school with a smile and a gift for me. I was disgusted. Why was he doing this to me? I asked myself. Why was he still loving me? How could he love a deformed woman? I didn't want his love. I was tired of being thankful for his continuing to love me despite the fact that I had no vagina. No man could love a woman who didn't have a uterus and a vagina. No man. Why didn't he just go away now and get it over with? That way I wouldn't have to wonder anymore or be grateful for his presence anymore. Just get it over with.

One day Mike called and I told him brutally that I didn't want him to come over. So he didn't come that night. And I cried. But the next night, there he was again. He held me and told me that things were going to work out and that he loved me. I told him I hated him, didn't love him, and never wanted to see him again. I told him he was ugly, stupid, and nasty. I hit him, punched him, screamed at him, and tormented him until we were both in tears. And so it went on. When I was being particularly aggressive, Mike would get up and leave. Then I was convinced that I had been right all along. You see, it's true, no one can love me now! But after a few days, Mike would call and he would be back.

After weeks of riding this emotional roller-coaster of hating Mike and hating myself I finally realized that he *could* love me, that he *did* love me, and, most important of all, that I could still be lovable. After such misery this revelation was extraordinarily liberating. I trusted Mike once more and I stopped hating myself.

The rest of the spring and summer passed fairly uneventfully. As soon as I was feeling well enough to get around, I volunteered to work three days a week at Albert Einstein College Hospital. I wanted to go back as someone able to help others rather than as the person needing help. Then, in July, Mom agreed to let me go on a vacation to California. I went with Mike and we stayed with his relatives in Los Angeles. The trip was very much needed and, being our first vacation together, very special.

Two things were significant about this time. The first was a conversation that my mother and I had with a friend of mine regarding DES. My mother told us that she felt so bad about the fact that the drug she had taken had caused all these problems for me. She said that she felt guilty. I reminded her that she had taken the DES to "save her pregnancy" with me, so that she wouldn't miscarry. I told her I knew that she would never, ever do anything to harm me. Mom said that she couldn't help feeling bad about it and that she would never forget how it had caused her daughter to suffer. I felt her pain, and I knew that there was nothing I could do to ease it, just as there was nothing she could do really to erase what had happened to me.

The other thing was that Dr. Daniel decided not to do the vaginal reconstruction at this time. I had been left with the lower third of my vaginal tissue (it was like a dimple), and he thought he could first try to stretch that tissue before considering any more surgery. Although I didn't really like the idea of stretching, I was more than glad to try something that might prevent me from having to go back to the hospital for another operation. I was already having nightmares about that second surgery. The dreams were vivid and frightening. I saw myself on the gurney again and being taken into surgery. I could imagine the pain. I would never forget the real pain. So I jumped at the option of trying an alternative to surgery. Dr. Daniel wasn't sure it would work. It was a technique that had only been used on young girls who had been born without vaginas, not on people like me. What I had to do was use plastic dilators—actually they were cylindrical molds—starting off with very small, narrow ones and working slowly up to larger, wider ones. Dr. Daniel explained that I would use these dialators to put pressure on my vaginal opening and keep pressure on it over time until the tissue slowly stretched and expanded. He told me that vaginal tissue is very elastic and can be stretched in this fashion, but that it was a time-consuming procedure and had to be done every morning and evening for an hour at a time over the course of almost a year. He suggested that we try it now and if there was no change by the time I returned from California, then we would talk about having the reconstructive surgery. I was determined it would work.

By the end of the summer, this method did seem to be working. It was an uncomfortable procedure. I knew that my vagina would never be as "normal" as other women's, but there was hope it would be functional. Reconstructive surgery had its risks, and anyway, that could be done at any time, if necessary. Dr. Daniel and I agreed: No reconstructive surgery, and I'd continue with the dilators.

In September it was back to Stony Brook once again. I moved into a suite with Rosey and many of my old friends. The year before, I had gone off young, fresh, and naive. This year I went off feeling much older, much wiser, and much more somber. Other people my age seemed younger and more immature. They were concerned with trivial matters, such as grades, hairstyles, and what movies to see. I was so serious. I felt I had really seen what life is like and it didn't come close to the sheltered, secure atmosphere of university life. I had experienced hardship, I had seen my own death, and most importantly, I had survived. Little things wouldn't upset me anymore. I would enjoy each day for whatever it would bring. At least I would try.

CHAPTER 7

The fact of the matter, though, was that things did upset me—perhaps not the minor annoyances of everyday life, but an awareness that started building in me as soon as I began to realize that I was going to live through this crisis.

Conversations with the doctors kept coming back to me while I lay in bed at night. Was my cancer related to Dad's previous problems? No, I had heard repeatedly from the specialists. No, it wasn't. Then why? Why did this happen to me? As I lay there in bed, I thought little about school or classes. I thought about the word I had heard: DES, diethylstilbestrol. I thought about the question I had been asked while in the hospital. "Did your mother take anything during her pregnancy with you?"

"Yes, Mom was given DES."

Ah-hah—a knowing look. It didn't seem to matter then, but it mattered now.

My mother was given a drug that she took to help save me, to keep me because she loved me even before I was born, and this same drug had almost destroyed me. I couldn't yet think about how this could happen. It was just sinking in that it did happen. The anger was there, but it did not surface. I could not think further about it. I tried to sleep.

On my next visit to Dr. Daniel for a check-up, I was jolted by something he said. He casually mentioned that I was part of the Herbst Registry. I asked what that was about. He explained that it was Dr. Arthur Herbst from Massachusetts General Hospital who had made the connection between DES and this type of cancer just the year before. Herbst was now keeping a registry of all known cases of this cancer from around the world. I was number seventy.

My heart raced. Again DES and my cancer. I was shocked that I had something that only seventy other women in the world were known to have. I was appalled that as many as seventy woman had suffered as I had suffered. This information was stored, I did not want to ask any more questions about it.

I was home from school for Thanksgiving dinner. It was a small family gathering. Of course Mike was there too. He was very much a part of the family now. Everyone was saying how thankful they were that I was there, that I was alive. Yes, I was thankful, too. Someone mentioned that it was terrible that a drug given to a mother so many years earlier could later have such devastating effects on her child. Yes, it was terrible, we all agreed. Someone mentioned that there had been a newspaper article about this drug suggesting that it had never been properly tested before being put on the market.

Something clicked in my mind as a strong sense of injustice and anger came to the fore. For the very first time I thought that perhaps we should take legal action, and I said so. To my surprise everyone looked knowingly at each other. It was evidently not a new thought to them. They had all been thinking about it before but hadn't wanted to say anything to me. I guess the victim is always the last to know. But right then and there we all agreed to pursue it just to see what the possibilities were. I didn't know who we would sue or how. My cousin Steven was an attorney for the Bronx District Attorney's office. Mom said she would call him the next day and talk it over with him.

Steve was very encouraging. He thought we should definitely pursue it, and he referred us to some attorneys in the area. We went to see one of them, who said he thought the case had merit but that his firm didn't have the resources to take it on. He referred us to someone else. After a few months we were finally referred to the firm of Julien, Schlesinger and Finz. David Jaroslawicz was an attorney with the firm. He met with us. His firm would take us on, but he explained that it was a "complicated" case and would take a while. We would have to be patient. He explained that as with all their product liability cases of this kind, they would take it on a contingency basis. That meant that we would have to pay one-third of our award if we won, and nothing if we lost.

The case was in their hands now. Life went on for me and not much thought was given to when the case would come up. It would take a while. I would deal with it later.

Life at school went on. I was enjoying college again. I was more serious about my classes than I had been the year before. I became involved in studying sociology and psychology and worked toward an interdisciplinary degree in social sciences.

As much as I enjoyed the weekdays, I couldn't wait for the weekends to arrive. That's when I would see Mike. It was amazing that we could have been through so much and still be in love. But we were. More so than ever. Mainly because we had shared so much together, much more so than most people our age. It was very special to us that we had shared that experience. No one else could ever understand when they found out that I had had cancer or surgery. Mike knew. We didn't really talk about it much. We didn't have to because it was part of both of us. I loved Mike partly because I knew he was someone I could count on.

We had the most beautiful weekends together. Either I would go to the city for the weekend and we would have fun exploring it, or Mike would come to Stony Brook and we'd take advantage of campus activities.

Mike was busy in school full-time himself (he was going to Lehman College) and was studying to be a speech pathologist. But we both always managed to get our work done during the week and would have the weekends entirely for each other.

During the week I missed him so much it hurt. We'd spend hours on the phone to each other, sharing our daily experiences and concerns, planning our futures, and expressing our love for each other. Weekdays were for school, friends, and contacts with others, but weekends were for Mike.

The routine of my college life was periodically broken up by trips into New York to see Dr. Daniel or Dr. Charlton. For a time after my surgery I would see one or both of them every three months, but soon it was every six months. These follow-up visits would always cause me extreme anxiety. Somehow, the in-between times were periods when my cancer could be covered over, denied, forgotten. I rarely spoke of it to anyone, and when I did, it was in vague, unclear terms. It was too painful. I did not want to discuss it. But each time I had to go to the doctor I could no longer deny the reason I was going. He was going to check to make sure the cancer hadn't returned. As good as I felt, I was reminded that I was not out of the woods yet.

The day of the appointment I would always lose my appetite, become very crabby, and pace anxiously. Once in the doctor's office I would nervously wait my turn to be called, unable to concentrate even on the magazines available to kill the time. On the examining table, with legs up, I would feel so sad. I would feel a heaviness about my being that I had difficulty explaining.

The doctor would insert the cold speculum. It was always the smallest one made since there was so little left of my vagina. Even that small speculum would have difficulty staying in. Then there was always a very

79

tense moment for me, when the doctor would hold the speculum in place and take his first look into my vagina. My heart always beat hard as he looked carefully and then palpated the vaginal walls. I would hardly listen to the small talk being made and would politely but briefly answer questions.

The next step was the iodine solution that was coated onto my vaginal walls. This iodine stain was painless but important in that if there were any abnormal cells, they would not take the stain the way the normal cells did and the doctor would see it immediately. The stain was on. The doctor peered in as I held my breath. "Looks beautiful!" he would say enthusiastically.

I'd let my breath out and say, "Really?"

"Couldn't be better. Everything looks good."

Then, for the first time, I would smile, feeling relieved and comfortable enough to converse with the doctor. I'd of course have to wait for the results of the special Pap* test they always took, but at this point I always felt that I was out of the woods, at least for the next six months. This routine would be repeated twice every year, with absolutely no exceptions. I was told that because of my DES exposure I would need to have these check-ups twice a year for the rest of my life. They were quick and painless, but I could never relax until after they were over.

Meanwhile, school went well for both Mike and me. Stony Brook life was quickly coming to an end. I was graduating Phi Beta Kappa with a B.A. in social sciences and had finally decided to pursue a career in social work. I had become interested in working with the elderly after having done some volunteer work in this area the year before. Mike had also graduated with honors and wanted to get his Masters in speech pathol-

---

* Usually a Pap test is a smear from the cervix. In my case, the doctor had to take a sample from the vaginal wall.

ogy. After a long, agonizing application procedure we were both accepted to the University of Michigan in Ann Arbor. It was a good choice for us both. The university had an excellent Masters of social work program as well as an excellent speech pathology program. We were excited about the move away from New York to this totally unfamiliar region.

Graduate school was challenging, and a lot more work than I had expected. It took a while to adjust, that first semester. There were so many things going on. I was excited about my first field placement for my social work degree. It was fun to go out there and really *be* a social worker.

Mike and I were now living together and although we had felt we knew everything there was to know about one another, it certainly was an adjustment to be actually living in the same apartment—especially since the apartment was tiny and both of us were a bit tense from all our schoolwork.

But with many ups and downs in between, we worked our little problems out and in March of 1976 we flew back to New York and got married. It was a simple ceremony, and Mike's Uncle Phil performed the services. The day after our wedding we were back at school again. We were both very happy, but it was a little strange, having known Michael for so long, to think of him as my husband instead of as my boyfriend. After having been Joyce Bichler for so many years, I couldn't see changing it, so we were now Joyce Bichler and Michael Kimbarow, Mr. & Ms.

The days went on, and we really never did think much about our pending legal suit. Occasionally, however, a call would come from the attorneys in New York saying that the trial was to begin in a few weeks and that I should get ready to come in for it. I'd begin to get anxious over it and complete all the arrangements, clear a leave of absence from school, and be all set to go, when another call would come, saying that, after all, there had been a delay. The trial was indefinitely postponed.

I became convinced that this trial would absolutely never get off the ground, though I realized that I wasn't really too upset about it. The thought of going to trial was really very frightening and I was in no rush to jump into it. The knowledge that I would someday have to do it did hang over our heads, but I preferred that to actually having to deal with going through the real thing.

After two good years at Michigan, Mike and I had to decide what we wanted to do from there. We were both finishing up our programs and pretty much had an open choice as to where to go to start our professional careers. Mike was graduating six months before me, so he sent out applications all around the country. When he got the job offer from San Francisco we nearly jumped out of our skins. Wouldn't it be so exciting to live in San Francisco? It was far from home, but Mike did have relatives in Southern California, so at least there would be some family not too far away. We had both fallen in love with the city the summer we had spent out in California after my surgery. We were exhilarated now by the thought of living there.

As soon as I finished with school we packed up our few belongings and took off for the West Coast. It took us time to settle in, but once we did we loved it. I found a wonderful job working with the elderly in a community day center right in the heart of Chinatown. Mike went through a period of dissatisfaction with his first job but then changed jobs and enjoyed his work as a speech pathologist in a hospital, working with people who had had head injuries or strokes. Life had never been better. We pined for our families in New York but always managed to arrange a trip back east when the homesickness got too bad. We were really feeling settled in.

One day while we were driving up for a camping weekend in northern California, I switched the radio on and heard a woman named Nancy Adess, who was talking about DES. I was frozen for a second but immediately interested. We turned up the radio. The woman was talking about the effects of DES, why you should ask your mother if she took anything during her pregnancy, and how you should go to a doctor who is knowledgeable about DES screening procedures to have a simple yet special examination. She then spoke of her organization, DES Action. It was a part of a national group, and there was a local DES Action group in San Francisco. The group promoted education about DES as well as provided support for those who had been affected by this drug. She gave the phone number. I took it down on a scrap of paper. Mike was enthusiastic and encouraged me to call as soon as we got back from our weekend. I wasn't ready yet, I thought. I put the number in a safe place in my purse, thinking that when we returned home I would then decide whether or not to call. Once the phone number was put away, it was never taken out again.

It was a year later, in April 1979, that I received another one of those "Come in for the trial" phone calls. This one was different. It was from Sybil Shainwald, an attorney with the Julien firm whom I had never met. She said she was now working on my case and that we would be going to court in three weeks. Sybil sounded sincere, but I just didn't believe it was finally happening. It had been *seven* years since I had decided to sue. I found out later that the firm had worked long and hard those seven years to put my case together. The time was spent putting together evidence, witnesses, testimony. The amount of detail work was monumental, but my legal team, meticulously and relentlessly, searched out every aspect of information and fact, and prepared a brilliantly documented and researched case. I had thought that the preparation would never end—that the trial would never happen. But here was Sybil insisting that this time we would actually get to court. I think she was surprised that I didn't sound excited or very enthused. All I could say was, "Are you sure, are you sure?" I didn't want to be caught up in the same spurt of emotion this time, just to be let down again.

"This is it," Sybil said. "Plan to be in New York for approximately three weeks."

That night I discussed it with Mike. "How can I leave my job for three whole weeks?" I said while pacing around the kitchen. "That's such a long time!" I continued pacing, alternating between the kitchen and the living room. "I have responsibilities, commitments. I can't just leave them all. I don't even know if I'll be able to get the time off! Who has the money to just fly off to New York? This is ridiculous, I won't be able to go. They'll just have to postpone it." Mike looked up at me as if I were crazy. "Wait a minute," he said, "this is something that we've been waiting for for seven years. This is your opportunity to fight back, to get retribution from those who were responsible for all that you've been through. You've been waiting for this moment for so long. I know it's frightening, but you have to do it. You know that you will do it. Everything else is secondary."

I took a moment to stop pacing. He was right. I did want to go through with it. It would be my chance to stand up and fight. I was scared, but I would do it. This was it.

The next day I went into work and arranged to take a three-week leave of absence.

A few days later I spoke to Sybil again, firming up the plans for my arrival in New York. In the course of the conversation, Sybil asked if Mike would be free to come in also. She said that it was important that he be there too.

That night I told Mike about this. This time it was he who started pacing and grumbling about how he couldn't take the time off from work and just drop everything else. This time I laughed and told him that this was what we were waiting for and that he knew he would do it. After he had done some more pacing, we finally agreed that I would go to New York first and then, when things got underway, Mike would follow.

PART TWO

CHAPTER 8

The flight back to New York was a long one. I don't like flying very much and I found it especially difficult to relax at this time. I kept thinking about how exciting it would be to see my family again, but I was also thinking about how I did not want to go through with the trial. What would the next weeks bring? I knew that so much would be happening. So much that I had no control over. I was confused. I really did want the trial, but I was afraid that I wouldn't be able to go through all that would be asked of me. Would I be able to stand up in a courtroom and testify? If I had to, I would, wouldn't I? Well, I'd find out soon enough.

If only Mike could be here now, I thought. I didn't want for him to join me later. I could do it on my own if I had to. I really wanted those drug companies to have to answer to me for what they had done. This is it, I thought, this is my chance. I think I can do it.

Getting off the plane it was wonderful to look around and have everyone there. Even my nephews, Andrew and Travis, and my niece Tracy. Lots of hugs and kisses. It felt good to be home.

I would be staying with my parents. They had recently moved into a house with my sister, brother-in-law, and nephew. They are all living now in West Nyack, New York, which is approximately twenty miles north of New York City.

My parents and I went into Manhattan to meet with the attorneys. I finally met Sybil, and she explained what would be happening. Mr. Julien, she said, was going to handle my case. It was going to be a two-part trial. In the first part we had to prove who manufactured the DES that my mother took. Some years before, my mother had telephoned the pharmacist who had supplied her with the pills to ask if he still had any of his own records. But apparently the pharmacy records had been lost long ago in a fire. The pharmacist, Mr. Willing, told my mother over the telephone that he remembered that during the 1950s he "only used Lilly, the best." So trial one would be to establish in court that Eli Lilly & Co. was the manufacturer of the DES that my mother took. Trial two, which would follow immediately after trial one, would go one of two ways. If the jury accepted the fact that Lilly was the manufacturer, then we would proceed from there, with Lilly as the defendant. If we couldn't prove Lilly as the manufacturer, then we would still proceed with Lilly as the defendant, only this time the theory behind the suit would be different. We would proceed on a joint product liability theory, which contends that even though we couldn't prove who manufactured the DES ingested by my mother, the pharmaceutical companies were all equally responsible for the damage since they acted together in getting this drug approved. Thus, we could sue Eli Lilly basically as a representative of all the drug companies that were involved in manufacturing the drug, particularly since Lilly was the major manufacturer of DES. As you can see, this theory is more complicated, and we were told that it had never been done this way before. Our case rested on the first trial and establishing that it was indeed Eli Lilly that manufactured the DES.

It was certainly a lot for us to digest, but we had plenty of time to think about it because Mr. Julien, who was supposed to be handling the case, was still involved in another trial. We had to wait until he was finished, but we were reassured that would be any day now.

Back we all went to West Nyack to think it through. I wasn't happy with this approach to the case. I didn't like it because it was clear that the burden and pressure rested firmly on the shoulders of my parents. Basically it would come down to my mother's testimony on her memory of what this pill that she took twenty-six years ago looked like and also what the pharmacist told her (which she remembered clearly). I knew Mom would be fine, but she was frightened of having to go on the stand and have this all fall on her. It didn't seem fair. This was my trial, my decision to go through with it, and I hadn't anticipated how much pressure and involvement would fall on my parents. They were so good. Actually they were all for the trial also. Mom had always felt so terrible about taking this pill that had caused me to have cancer, even though she knew that she had taken it only because she had wanted to have me so badly. Still, it was a difficult thing for her to deal with. She was also angry about how this pill had not been tested properly, and she wanted the drug company to take responsibility for it.

Meanwhile, Mr. Julien's trial kept going on. The weeks were passing quickly. The delays were getting frustrating. His trial was taking much longer than expected. I kept getting annoyed as each day passed. Two weeks were already gone, and to think I'd imagined I'd only be away from my job for three weeks. We hadn't even gotten started yet. Mike had come in as scheduled, but it seemed for nothing. As the days wore on, there was talk about postponing the trial until after the summer. I was so upset! They did it to me again—I had gotten up and excited for the trial all for nothing! How terribly unfair.

Just as I was getting used to the idea that the trial wouldn't happen this time, I received another call from the attorneys. The trial was to go ahead after all, but instead of Mr. Julien, who was still tied up with his other trial, another partner, Mr. Leonard Finz, would handle the case. I had grave reservations about this news. Mr. Julien was my attorney, he was supposed to handle my case. That was how it had been planned for the past seven years. Who was this Mr. Finz, anyway?

Apparently Finz had been a New York Supreme Court justice for the past twelve years and was, in fact, still referred to as Judge Finz. He had recently voluntarily stepped down to resume the practice of law. This was all very impressive, I thought, but it wasn't good enough. My case had been with Mr. Julien for seven years; he was the one to do it, and no one else would do.

I was petulant about this matter for some days, but then it became clear that if I didn't go with Judge Finz, then the trial would definitely be postponed again, as the court would wait for Mr. Julien no longer. Mr. Julien would try my case if he could, but of course he could not walk out on the case he was currently in the midst of trying. All the members of my family had reservations about the change, too, but they knew it had to be my decision, and they said little to me about it.

I realized there was no point in postponing it again. I really had no reason at all to doubt Judge Finz—it was just that it was a change, and that scared me. I couldn't go through the anguish of waiting longer or the hassle of stopping my life for the trial again. It had to be now or never. We would go with Judge Finz, I decided. There was to be no turning back now.

Mike and I went to the law offices together to meet with Judge Finz for the first time. I was nervous about the encounter, mainly because I still wasn't really happy about him handling my case. I didn't know what Judge Finz would expect from me, but I was determined to be open and honest and go from there.

We arrived at the office looking a lot more disheveled than we would have liked because we had been caught in a sudden rain shower on the way. I felt even more self-conscious than before. We sat in the reception area for a while, until we were ushered into an office and told that Judge Finz would be with us in a minute. The office walls were heavy with impressive-looking awards, trophies, and plaques. They were very imposing and we were awed into virtual silence while we waited. After ten minutes, in came Judge Finz. He was a distinguished-looking, middle-aged man. He had dark hair and a real gleam in his brown eyes. He shook our hands and introduced himself as Leonard Finz. Behind him walked Sybil (I was glad to see a familiar face), and they called in another attorney who had been working on the case but whom I had not met before—Ed Sanocki.

We all took our seats. Judge Finz sat behind his enormous desk and proceeded to tell us a little about himself. He explained that he had been a Supreme Court justice for twelve years and had seen everything from both sides of the bench. He told us about how he had voluntarily left the bench to resume an active practice because that was what he enjoyed doing most. Then he told us about his very successful track record. In fact, he said, he had only just left a very happy Brooklyn man whose case had finally been settled for a tidy sum of money. He hoped this made me feel reassured. I think, instead, that I felt overwhelmed; the man was such a ball of energy. I hardly felt reassured. Indeed, I was getting more nervous.

Next, Judge Finz went over the procedures of the trial. Basically he repeated what Sybil had told us earlier about it being a two-part trial. He stressed the fact that if we didn't win the first part, we would be in a more difficult situation, but he did seem confident that we could indeed show that it was Lilly that manufactured the DES my mother took.

Judge Finz asked Mike and me some questions about our feelings regarding the case. He asked how the surgery had affected my life. I quickly gave him a brief and unemotional response about how I couldn't have children and had suffered greatly. I could tell that I was

93

expected to be more specific than that. The defenses came up and I got tense. I had never spoken about my surgery before a group of strangers like this.

I rarely told anyone about what had happened to me. Even friends I had known for several years were not aware of the nature of my surgery. Occasionally, if someone asked if I could give them a tampon, I was forced to explain that I had had a hysterectomy, but only the people I had known during the time I was in the hospital knew I had had a vaginectomy. I never could talk about it. It was hard for me even to think about it myself. There was an enormous store of feelings about my surgery that I had tucked away and never dealt with. I knew that one day I would have to let them all out, but I was afraid of the uncontrollable flood of emotions that was there. Occasionally, some of these feelings had crept out. For example, every now and then I'd be watching television and a commercial for baby diapers or baby food would come on and there would be a tiny, cute infant being held tenderly by its mother. How nice, I'd automatically think, can't wait to be pregnant and have mine. The hard truth would then flash in my mind, reminding me that I was dreaming. No, that won't happen to you. Not *ever!* The words would haunt me. Invariably, I'd end up sitting in front of the television feeling very choked up, with tears streaming down my cheeks. But never for long. I always swallowed hard and pushed those feelings back down again. I never let them go any further. I never allowed myself to express them fully.

Another time I was particularly vulnerable was when I had to go for my six-months' check-up. I would sit and stare at all the pregnant women in the doctor's office and alternate between being fascinated by them and being angry at them. I always felt uncomfortable there, but I chose not to examine the feelings that prompted my thoughts.

The most frightening experience I had of this sort occurred in 1976, while I was in my Master's program. A friend and fellow social work student, Charlotte, was describing a workshop she and her husband had been involved in. The workshop was designed to help couples understand their feelings about each other. Charlotte described to me and two other students one of the exercises that encouraged the couples to examine themselves and their lives and to assess the importance of each partner in the other's life. Charlotte told us how her husband had to imagine he was on his deathbed. He had to imagine the last things he would be saying to his wife. As Charlotte described the scene in great detail, I began to see the deathbed, I could see the oxygen tanks. I suddenly saw myself in room 914 of Albert Einstein College Hospital, and Mike was there.

I moved away from the others. Charlotte was still talking as I started to cry. I felt it was I who was dying. I couldn't stop myself from being very emotional, and suddenly the others were around me, trying to find out what was the matter.

It took me some time to calm down and shake off that terrifying image of death. It had scared me and also indicated clearly that I had never truly come to terms with my illness. My friends encouraged me to seek counseling to help bring all this to the surface. I knew they were right and I knew that I should take advantage of the university's counseling services while I was still there, but I made excuses not to. I didn't want to stir anything up. I was functioning all right, apart from those few instances and occasional nightmares. I was too scared. It would hurt too much, and I wasn't ready to deal with the hurt again, not then.

But now, seven years later, I was being forced to face it. Judge Finz was going to mention the unmentionable, the Big Hurt, the thing that even Mike and I only alluded to and never really discussed again after my return from the hospital. I knew the question was coming: "Tell me about the vaginectomy. How has that affected your relationship with Michael?"

Everyone was looking at me. I had to answer. I could feel myself turning beet red, and I didn't know where to look. I didn't know what to say or how to start. "Perhaps Ed and I should leave," Sybil suggested tactfully. "No," said Judge Finz, "I think you should stay. What do you think, Joyce?"

Feeling even more embarrassed now that the issue was my embarrassment, I said they should stay. I told myself that I would have to get used to talking about all this, if only because of the trial. I took a deep breath and began. I mumbled, and ranted, and burbled about how of course the vaginectomy has affected my life and our relationship, and how things aren't normal, and how I feel guilty and although my vagina is stretched, sex has never really been right. I was convinced that no one understood a word; I didn't even know myself what I was talking about. I wasn't very lucid. All I could do was allude to all the pain and hurt I had suffered with regard to sexuality. I wasn't clear. I couldn't explain. I couldn't explain because I had never put those feelings into words, not even to myself.

Yet I did want them to know. It was important, it was the truth, it was the core of what DES had done to me. For the first time, I got a glimpse of what going to trial was to mean. If I wanted to present to a jury the true picture of what had happened to me, then the time to deal with my feelings and evaluate the real effects of that surgery was now. There could be no more putting it off.

Judge Finz didn't press me for more information at this time. Just from my composure (or lack of it) he could tell that my vaginectomy had had serious consequences for me. He went on to say what Mike and I had already agreed on: That there was absolutely no need to sensationalize the trial, there was no need to play up any issues at all. The basic truth, he said, was enough. I believed this too, because I was still as concerned with honesty as I had been while I was in the hospital. But Judge Finz went on. In front of us all he gave an eloquent speech about Truth, Justice, and the American Way and how all we needed was the truth and if that wasn't enough to win a case in this country, then he wouldn't be practicing law. I really wanted to believe him, but I did have a few doubts about whether that was the way our legal system really operated. I was determined to uphold these values, but how could I be sure that the other side would too? Here I was, little Joyce Bichler, fighting Eli Lilly & Co., one of the major pharmaceutical companies in the world. Judge Finz believed that the truth would win. We would all just have to wait and see.

Although shook up by this meeting, I left feeling impressed with Judge Finz. He was strong, sincere, and although direct, I sensed a great deal of sensitivity. In fact, as nervous as I was about going to trial, I felt so good to be represented by the three people in that room: Judge Finz, Sybil and Ed. So far the firm had been extremely good to me. Their offices were all filled to overflowing with files and papers regarding my case: Seven years of work and absolutely no money exchanged. This was purely a contingency case—they got nothing unless I won something. And there were certainly no guarantees in this case. I wanted to express some thanks, but didn't know how. Instead, Mike and I scurried out.

My case was of great importance to all DES daughters around the country. I, at least, was getting the opportunity to go to court. The statute of limitations in many states and the problem of identification had prevented others from bringing to trial their cases, since with DES the harmful agent had usually been taken at least twenty years before any ill-effects were seen. Such cases were thrown out even before they saw the inside of a courtroom. New York State's laws are particularly restrictive. Of all the hundreds of cases that were pending, only two cases had ever come to trial, and out of these, one had lost and the other had ended after pitifully small settlements had been offered. Most settlements were offered after the case had already gone to the jury, and in one heartbreaking situation the woman had accepted a settlement, only to find that the jury would have come back unanimously in her favor if she had only had the strength to wait it out. This information impressed me. I realized that this was *not* an individual issue—it was a DES issue, a women's health issue—and the outcome of my case would have far-reaching consequences. I decided that either the drug company would have to offer an amount that indicated they were ready to admit that they were wrong, or I would fight them to the very end, win or lose.

The weekend before the trial on Monday there was a total shifting of gears. My brother, Dennis, was getting married. Concern about the trial had almost pushed out the happy anticipation of this family event. Almost, but not quite. It was Dennis' second marriage, and we were all very happy for him. His fiancée, Felice, was a terrific person, and one of the nice things about being in New York waiting for the trial to start was that I was able to spend some time with her.

The wedding took place on Saturday night in a small loft in mid-Manhattan. Dennis was nervous, Felice was beautiful, my mother was radiant. It was such an enjoyable wedding, but underneath my gaiety I couldn't help thinking about what the following week would bring. My nerves were also not calmed by the fact that every relative in attendance came up to ask what was happening on that front.

But the night was fun, and for the first time in weeks my mind was off myself.

CHAPTER 9

It was Monday, May 21, 1979. The first day of the trial. I woke early and dressed quickly. At breakfast, little was said. I wasn't the only nervous one.

The trial was to take place in the Bronx Supreme Court, which is close to Yankee Stadium. Immediately after breakfast, Mike and I drove down with my parents from West Nyack, and we were the first people to arrive in the courtroom. It was an extraordinarily impressive room, with wood paneling all around, high, imposing ceilings, and enormous chandeliers. It looked like something right out of "Perry Mason," which, of course, was my only source of information about how courts operated.

I suddenly realized that we were all whispering to each other, as though silence were really obligatory. We sounded ridiculous, but whispering did seem more appropriate than talking in normal tones, which resounded around the empty room. We sat down and anxiously waited for someone else to arrive.

At last Judge Finz came in, followed by Sybil and Ed. It was a relief to see their familiar faces in these awesome surroundings. Just as my mother was asking Judge Finz where we should all sit, the attorneys for Eli Lilly & Co. walked in. I froze. My parents turned to look. The attorneys had a huge entourage with them—people carrying all sorts of attaché cases and files. Eli Lilly's head attorney, Judge Finz had told us, was named Russel H. Beatie, Jr. I spotted him immediately. He was wearing a pin-striped suit, and, it seemed to me, anyway, that he had an arrogant expression on his face.

99

I glared at him. How could anyone defend such a case?
I thought angrily.

Judge Finz showed us where to sit. Instead of sitting
up at the table with my attorneys ("Perry Mason"
style), I had to sit with my family, directly behind the
table, and perpendicular to the jury box. At this point
the jury box was completely empty. I could hardly keep
my eyes off it. Everything depended on the people who
were presently going to be sitting in there. Everything.

Suddenly everyone in the courtroom stood up as the
judge's entrance was announced. Justice Arnold Guy
Fraiman was a thin, middle-aged man with gray hair in
a crew-cut. He wore a bow tie and long, black flowing
robes, which were just as intimidating as the austere
decor of the room. The trial had begun.

Since "Perry Mason" had molded my view of legal
trials, I had no idea that the procedure would take so
long. On "Perry Mason," the entire trial takes place
within one hour. How misguided I was. The whole of
that first day in the Bronx Supreme Court was spent
selecting the jury.

I had learned that since mine was a civil case, New
York State law required only six jurors rather than
twelve. A group of people were sent up from the jury
pool to the courtroom. I thought they were a motley
crew as they were directed to sit in the seats behind
us—men, women, young, old, well-dressed, and shabby.
Some of them actually looked as though they were
going off to the beach immediately after the recess.
Most didn't look particularly interested in what was
going on, but others looked surprisingly tense.

It was the time for the attorneys to question the
jurors and select those who were to end up sitting in
that jury box. I didn't think I would be so nervous at this
stage, but I was. I realized how crucial this selection
was. On one level I was glad that I didn't have to decide
who would be honest, unbiased—in short, a good juror;
what a responsibility. But on the other hand, I did feel I

wanted some control, some say in the matter. Looking at some of those people made me very uncomfortable; some were obviously unsuitable. But it was just a feeling, and there was little I could do except sit there and hope that Judge Finz felt it too. All I could do was sit, with Mike on my left, Mom on my right, and Dad to the right of her.

The court clerk put pieces of paper with the names of all the prospective jurors into a wooden box. The box had a handle that the clerk turned, mixing the names up. It was like a game of bingo. Then the clerk picked out six names from the box and called them out. Six people rose from their chairs and took seats in the jury box. It was just like a legal version of "The Price Is Right," but instead of Bob Barker calling out, "Come on down!" it was Charlie the court clerk.

Before the attorneys were given a chance to question these people, Justice Fraiman asked them each questions from a prepared list in front of him. He asked each one to look over at where we were sitting and announce whether they knew any of us or not. The prospective jurors were told to shake their heads as well as answer in loud voices when they responded to his questions. Anyone who didn't was quite severely reprimanded by Justice Fraiman. I felt glad that I could sit quietly down here as the plaintiff rather than up there as a juror. One question Justice Fraiman asked was whether anyone owned stock in Eli Lilly. Another was whether anyone had ever heard of DES. If someone said, "Yes," to any of these questions, he or she was sent back downstairs to the jury room to be picked for another trial. After several seats were emptied, Charlie then picked out some more names from the box and the "Come on down" routine continued, until all seats in the jury box were once again filled.

One thing I noticed while watching all this was that there were plenty of people who didn't want to sit on any jury. I noticed this when several of them, having seen how someone before them had got excused, would try to do the same. Justice Fraiman quickly became wise to that and lectured those in the jury box about one's civic duty to sit on a jury. The culprits were excused anyway, but the message went out loud and clear to the others waiting to be called that they had better play this game straight.

This was an incredibly boring procedure. At one point I found myself staring out of the windows and was amused to discover that I could see right into the stands of Yankee Stadium—it was that close. The hours dragged by, but there was one incident that did shake me.

While Justice Fraiman was questioning a new group of prospective jurors, I noticed the man sitting in seat number three. He looked restless and uncomfortable. When the justice told him to look over at our seats and say whether he recognized anyone, the man seemed very uneasy. It was as if he couldn't bear to look at either me or my family. He glanced quickly and then looked at the floor as he answered, "No." I couldn't figure out what was wrong with him. He answered, "No" to whether he owned any stock in Lilly, whether he knew any of the lawyers, and whether any of his relatives were doctors, but when Fraiman asked whether he had heard of DES, the man's whole manner changed. He stopped looking jittery and held his head up high as he answered a firm "Yes." Fraiman asked him in what capacity he had heard of it. In a clear, loud voice that rang across the courtroom, the man in seat number three said, "I have a DES daughter."

There was total silence. My mother and I looked at each other in astonishment. Justice Fraiman quickly said, "You are excused." The man stood up and walked out of the courtroom, all eyes upon him. I wanted to run after him, to talk to him, but instead I sat glued to my seat. It was only afterward that I realized that the scene could have been straight out of "Perry Mason."

The six seats were filled. Justice Fraiman had finished his questioning. Now the attorneys had their go at it. Judge Finz went first. He asked the prospective jurors whether they were married or unmarried, whether they had children, and what line of work they were in. He asked how they felt about big businesses, and about research on products sold to the public. From a long and tedious line of questioning Judge Finz would make a judgment on whether to excuse a juror or not. Each time someone was excused, and there was a new group in the box, Justice Fraiman had to question them before they were questioned by Judge Finz.

Finally Judge Finz was satisfied with the six in the box. Now it was Beatie's turn. He asked his own questions and excused people, just as Judge Finz had done. Every time a seat became empty, the procedure would be started all over again, as Charlie the court clerk called out a new name.

At last there were six jurors in the box, and two alternates, all chosen from this rigorous system of questioning. Although I had done nothing but sit throughout those hours, I felt exhausted, and here I was, facing the half-dozen people who were all important to me at that moment. I felt as though my fate were now in their hands.

Of the six jurors there were four women and two men; four were white, and two black. They were all middle-aged or older, and they seemed to be ordinary working-class people. Yet they had suddenly been thrown together to make an important decision in my life even though they had never met me before. It could go either way. I shuddered.

We broke for the day. The jurors were instructed by Justice Fraiman not to speak to me, my family, or any of the attorneys. They were told not to talk about the case with anyone. They were not even allowed to discuss it among themselves. They were told that if there was anything about the trial in any of the media, they should ignore it, whether on television, the radio, or in the newspapers. At last we recessed until the next day.

At home that evening, we all felt a little subdued, anxious about what lay so immediately ahead of us. Despite my nervousness, I slept soundly, and we were all up early again the next day.

Tuesday, May 22, 1979. We were back in our places in the courtroom on the second day of the trial. The jury had been picked; now it was time for the opening statements.

The attorney for each side used these statements to lay out the framework of his case. He told the jury the important points without revealing too much. For this part of the trial only one question was being asked: Was the DES that my mother took manufactured by Eli Lilly & Co.? There would be no discussion of cancer, negligence, or injury. It was a simple and straightforward case.

In his opening statement, Judge Finz laid it out clearly. We would be showing, he said, that Eli Lilly & Co. was the major manufacturer of DES during the 1950s when it was prescribed to my mother. We would also show that Lilly had been the absolute major supplier of DES to the pharmacies in the area of the Bronx in which my mother's prescription was filled, and that it had been economically more profitable for pharmacies to carry the more expensive Lilly product in their stores than the cheaper, lesser-known brands. Finally, he said, there was Mrs. Bichler's testimony detailing her conversation with Mr. Willing, the pharmacist who filled the prescription, and her memory of taking a round white pill.

Next it was Lilly's turn. Their opening argument was just as simple. Beatie claimed that all records for the period in question had been destroyed and that there was no way to prove that Lilly had the largest share of the DES market in the 1950s. He claimed that even small pharmacies had carried a variety of different manufacturers' products, and that there was no way Mr. Willing could have told my mother that he gave her a Lilly product.

So much for the opening statements. I felt agonizingly frustrated by Lilly's claims. I knew it was going to be hard to listen to their arguments since I knew that we were right and they were wrong. It was as simple as that. It seemed obvious to me that an enormous company like Eli Lilly couldn't just "accidentally" have destroyed its sales records for that period. But would the jury see that?

After the opening statements, the plaintiff's case is heard. Our first witness was from Eli Lilly & Co. itself. A Mr. Taylor, he had been an attorney for Lilly & Co. for thirty-one years. To me he appeared quite hostile, but Judge Finz handled him well. He was very reluctant to give out any information, but Finz managed to make him admit that Lilly certainly had been a major DES supplier during the period. This witness seemed to be on the stand for a long time, with the initial questioning, the cross-examination, and the re-examination. The seats in the courtroom could get very hard.

The day was soon over. I hadn't been looking forward to this day's end because Mike had to return to California. His vacation time was over, and one of us had to keep bringing in money to pay the bills. I hated to see him go. Just as I had so many years ago, I felt I needed him for emotional support. I was scared and frightened now, just as I had been then. Although this time I knew I could manage to go through this without him, I also knew it would be difficult not to have him there to lean on. We were both apprehensive about his departure. The trial was such an important event, and we knew it was going to be virtually impossible for me to describe each day's events to him over the telephone. But phone descriptions would have to do. Mike just couldn't afford to lose his job.

On the way home from the courtroom that night, we dropped Mike off at his parents' apartment. He was going to spend the night there so he could get to the airport early in the morning. We were sad to say goodbye; we really had no idea when we would see each other again.

The next days of the trial saw a series of witnesses, marketing researchers and local pharmacists, who described the marketing practices of the pharmaceutical companies in the Bronx during the early 1950s. Their testimonies were based on records they had seen, marketing research techniques, and extrapolation from existing figures, and they stated that Lilly was by far the major DES distributor to that small area of the Bronx.

A witness stated that Lilly was the industry's number one franchise for a wholesale distributor. Other witnesses called were pharmacists who had small pharmacies in that neighborhood. Some of them had their stores only a few blocks away from Mr. Willing's; they basically all served the same area. All these pharmacies gave similar accounts. They each claimed that Lilly had been the major distributor of DES during the 1950s, and that based on the cost and selling price of the Lilly product, it was more profitable for a small pharmacy to stock and sell it rather than other products. It was more profitable because if they had a 50 percent markup on their products, then there would be a larger profit on a more expensive product. It was stressed that the days of generic drugs and retail pharmacy outlets had not then arrived. These witnesses had had small stores with little space, so they could only have a limited stock. It was all very convincing to me.

One evening soon after the trial began I received a telephone call from the *New York Post*. They said they were going to run a story about the trial and were sending a photographer over to take a photograph of me and my mother. As I put down the receiver, I panicked. Judge Finz had warned me that there might be some publicity because I was the first DES daughter to sue in New York. Up until then, even though I knew my case was important for others, it had been a private matter. Now it was to become public. The *Post* was running a story and a photographer was on his way over. I had only just changed out of my tidy court clothes into my usual attire of jeans and t-shirt. Mom had also changed into a housedress. She must have heard me talking to the reporter and giving the photographer directions. By the time I had got off the phone, turned around, and screamed that a photographer from the *Post* was on his way over, Mom had already gotten dressed again.

We could hardly believe that our story was actually going to be in the newspapers. It seemed strange that others would be interested in what was happening to us. On one level it seemed like an invasion, but on the other it seemed that publicizing the case was something we had to do.

I called up Judge Finz to let him know what was happening. He said that it was entirely up to me to decide whether to talk to the newspapers. But of course no further decision was necessary; the photographer was already on his way over.

Every time a car rolled up the street, I jumped. I didn't like having my picture taken for anything, let alone a newspaper. I was extremely nervous, and we had to wait for over two hours before the photographer arrived. He had gotten lost. Finally the doorbell rang. The photographer came in, told my mother and me to sit down on the couch, took a few shots, and was gone. He wasn't there for more than ten minutes, and it was a silly thing to have been so jittery about.

The next day the story was out: "First Suit by DES Baby May Set Legal Standard." I felt very uncomfortable reading about myself in print, but I had a feeling that I was going to have to get used to it. I thought about all the other DES daughters in New York who might be reading this same article. I wondered what they were feeling as they did so. I knew we had to win the case, as much for them and all the other DES daughters in America as for myself. I knew I had a duty to win.

Mr. Willing was going to be the first witness called to the stand that day. We were all nervous about his testimony because it was so crucial, but I was sure that what he had to say would prove that we were right.

We all sat in our places. I held Mom's hand as Mr. Willing's name was called. My heart was thumping. Now the jury will see who is right, I thought. Now they have to see what happened twenty-six years ago.

My family had lived down the street from Mr. Willing's small neighborhood pharmacy for eighteen years. I had been too young to remember him, but the rest of the family had known Mr. Willing well. In fact, Dennis and Arlene had told me about how they always went into Mr. Willing's store whenever they had something in their eye, and he was always there to take it out. Mr. Willing had been a part of everyday neighborhood life, just as Dad, being the local fire inspector, had been. Dad knew Mr. Willing well, not only from being a customer but also because he had to fill out inspection papers in the store. In that neighborhood Dad had been known as the "fireman." Mom was frequently addressed not as Mrs. Bichler but as "Mrs. Fireman," or referred to as the "fireman's wife."

When Mom had spoken to Mr. Willing over the telephone to ask if he remembered who had manufactured the DES she'd been given, he had still remembered the nickname.

"This is Mrs. Bichler," Mom had said.

"How is your husband, the fireman?" Mr. Willing had asked.

When Mom told him how ill I had been, he had sounded quite upset and had said he regretted not being able to provide the records since they had been lost in a fire a few years before. But he had said, "I only used Lilly, the best."

I couldn't see what else Mr. Willing might say; it seemed so straightforward. However, I was a little worried because we had found out a year before that Mr. Willing was being represented by Dewey, Ballantine, Bushby, Palmer & Wood, the same attorneys who were representing Eli Lilly. That was odd anyway, and it also seemed very strange that an unknown pharmacist would be represented by such a large, expensive, and prestigious law firm.

Mr. Willing walked into the courtroom. He was an elderly gentleman with gray hair. He looked very grandfatherly. He took the stand and he swore to tell the truth. Mr. Willing told Judge Finz that he was eighty-six years old. He described his small neighborhood pharmacy. He said he had been there for many years.

My parents were then asked by Judge Finz to stand up and to walk right in front of Mr. Willing. Mom and Dad did as they were asked, and individually, one after the other, stood, no more than three feet away from him. Mr. Willing was asked first if he knew who my father was. There was complete silence as he looked at my father for a few seconds. Then he turned to look across the court. "Definitely not," he announced.

I couldn't believe he was saying that. I couldn't believe what he said as he continued. Mr. Willing told the court that he had never heard the name "Bichler," and then later in his testimony he said that he had never had a conversation on the phone with my mother.

I could see the hurt and frustration in my parents'

eyes. I shared their disbelief that this old man was saying all this. How could he? I shared their frustration; there was absolutely nothing they could do.

Mr. Willing went on to say that he could never have said he used Lilly. He had used many brands, he said. Although he ran a small pharmacy and he admitted that DES was not a fast-moving product, he stated that he had kept four or five different brands of DES stacked on the shelves. Therefore, he said, Mrs. Bichler could have had any one of those.

I could feel my parents' rage as Mr. Willing sat there and said those things. I could tell that my mother was trying to make eye contact with him, but, not surprisingly, Mr. Willing never was able to look her directly in the eye.

After his testimony, Mr. Willing immediately left the courtroom. We were left shattered. We never heard from Mr. Willing again.

That day was an important one in court. It was a day that would sting for a long time afterward because that was the day I saw my parents get hurt, the day in which I lost a little bit of faith in people.

I called Mike that night, I was so upset. He couldn't believe Willing had denied knowing my parents. Mike felt so bad he couldn't be there. I could feel his frustration and mine.

The next day in court was to be the most traumatic, at least during this part of the trial. It was the day my parents were called, individually, to testify from the witness stand. It was the day we had all been dreading, the one we were most anxious about.

My father was called to testify first. As he sat in the stand, I could hardly bear to look. Dad sat up there looking calmer than the way I felt. He spoke loudly and clearly. My heart went out to him as he sat in front of all those people and described the events that happened twenty-six years before. Guided by Judge Finz's questions, Dad told the court of how he had driven my mother to see Dr. Fleischer and then brought her home afterward. He said he had gone down to the pharmacy at the corner of the block, with Dr. Fleischer's prescription for Mom, and brought back the pills to her at home. He said he could not remember what the pills looked like. His testimony was short and simple and fortunately did not have to last too long. Beatie cross-examined him briefly about the container the pills were in. I didn't like the idea of Beatie even talking to my father, let alone questioning him in that accusatory, arrogant tone of his. But Dad stood his ground. I was glad when the questioning was over.

Now it was my mother's turn. Poor Mom was so nervous she could hardly stop shaking when she first went up to the stand. She had told me beforehand that she wasn't worried about what she had to say because it was, after all, only what she could remember, and that was the truth. She just didn't like the idea of getting up in that courtroom and answering so many questions, and she was particularly anxious about Mr. Beatie cross-examining her, since she knew he would do his best to challenge and confuse her. At the same time, she knew that she was the crucial witness, that so much depended on her.

When she first began answering Judge Finz's questions, her voice was soft and wavering but gradually it became clearer and stronger as she became more confident. Judge Finz was wonderful. I regretted all my earlier doubts about him handling the case. He told Mom many times that all she had to do was tell the truth, and he frequently reassured her that it didn't matter if she couldn't remember all the details of what had happened. Finz's gentle manner helped Mom relax and although I could tell she was still nervous, she slowly became calmer as she told the court her story.

Mom said that she had had some spotting when she was three months' pregnant in 1953, and her obstetrician, Dr. Fleischer, had given her a prescription for some drugs to stop her from miscarrying, to "help save the baby," he had said. She said that her husband had collected the pills for her from the pharmacy and brought them back. The pills, she said, were small, white, and round; she remembered them clearly. She had followed the doctor's instructions and taken the pills for twelve days. After all these details, Mom then explained how in 1973, after I had had my surgery, she had called the pharmacist who had given her husband the pills to ask him what drug company had supplied him with them. Mom stated that the pharmacist, Mr. Willing, had told her over the telephone that the pills must have come from Eli Lilly & Co., and that he had said, "I only used Lilly, the best."

Judge Finz questioned Mom very closely about this and she insisted, over and over again, that everything had happened exactly as she had said. Finally, Finz asked if she would swear on her daughter's life that Mr. Willing had actually said those words to her. Mom (who normally never swears) straightened herself up and said, in a clear voice that carried across the courtroom, "Yes, I swear on my daughter's life that Mr. Willing said that he only used Lilly, the best."

Now it was Mr. Beatie's turn to question Mom. He stood up and sauntered across to the witness stand. For a second, I though Mom actually recoiled as he approached, but then she looked straight at him, almost defiantly. I was so proud of her.

Beatie tried to do whatever he could to shake Mom's testimony. He showed her different pills and asked if she remembered such things as cross-hatches, names, or other marks inscribed on the pills she took. He asked her to describe exactly the size, shape, and type of bottle that the pills were in. Mom told him that she couldn't remember most of the things he wanted to know. She told him over and over again what she did remember from that time. She stood up to Beatie's grilling very well. She refused to get flustered or be intimidated by him, despite his effort. She just told him, as simply as possible, everything she did know.

By the end of the day, Beatie had finished his cross-examination. What a relief! I was exhausted. Although it was Mom and Dad who had had to perform, to talk in front of everyone, to stand up to the barrage of questions, I almost felt as though I had gone through all that myself. And I hadn't realized that the trial would be so taxing on my parents. It seemed ironic that although it was I who was suing, I hadn't had to testify at all. All I'd had to do was get on the stand for a minute and acknowledge that I was indeed Joyce Bichler, daughter of Dorothy and Max Bichler.

As we drove home that evening it was obvious that we were all drained. But at least we had done all we could; our case had been presented. Now we had to see what arguments Lilly would put forward. I knew it wasn't going to be pleasant listening to them, but I was ready.

I couldn't wait to get home and telephone Mike that evening. He wanted to know all that was happening, in detail. Every time I'd tell him something he'd say, "Yeah, and then what happened?" and I'd go on and on trying to remember all the important events. The days were so long and packed with so much excitement and information that it was hard to remember everything, but I tried.

Despite my mental preparations for Lilly's arguments in their defense, I still found them infuriating. For everything we had presented they presented the opposite information. They called other pharmacists to the stand to testify that it was not more profitable to stock Lilly products during the 1950s. They took the same books that we had presented to show that the profit margin was higher on Lilly products than on others and then said that if you read the figures a certain way it

113

wasn't in fact true. We had brought in other pharmacists from the Bronx; Mr. Beatie brought his witnesses in from Manhattan. For absolutely everything we had argued, Lilly had a counterargument. It went back and forth, back and forth. It was so painful to have to sit there and listen. I was almost squirming with rage at times. But through all this I still believed that the jurors would see the truth, that they would find in our favor. They had to. My tremendous faith in those six people helped me keep up my strength throughout the ordeal.

CHAPTER 10

After two weeks, the trial was drawing to an end. Now it was time for the closing arguments. These summarized all that had been said over the course of the trial. They tied up all the loose ends and the attorneys made their last points.

The defense went first. Mr. Beatie emphasized that it had not been profitable for small pharmacists to stock only Lilly products and that therefore my mother could have been given any one of a number of different brands of DES.

After Beatie, Judge Finz gave his closing statement. He reiterated all the points our side had made. Then he pointed out to the jury that this was a civil rather than a criminal case. In a civil case it does not have to be proved beyond a reasonable doubt that something is true; it just has to be shown that the evidence is weighted toward one side or the other. It was important to let the jurors know that they could still find that my mother's DES was a Lilly product even though there might not be any specific evidence "proving" that it was.

It was a long process. The whole day was taken up with the closing statements. We recessed. The jury was to be charged the next day and would start their deliberations. Although I had felt shaky throughout the trial, at this point I was actually feeling more confident than ever. Judge Finz had presented a great case. It seemed so evident that any good businessman would use a Lilly product in those days. And certainly, despite Mr. Willing's denials, my mother's testimony had been very convincing. I wasn't the only one feeling good.

Judge Finz, Sybil, and Ed all thought we had it locked up. They didn't say that directly, but I could just tell that they were optimistic. Mom and Dad also sensed that, and they felt good. Another reason for my buoyant mood was that Mike was returning the next morning. Judge Finz had thought it time to call Mike back east for the jury's decision. We all thought we had a victory here and either way, we would be going directly into the second part of the trial immediately afterward. It had been two weeks since Mike had left, and I had really missed him, despite our regular telephone conversations. At this point, too, I think we were all hoping that when we won this section, Lilly would feel it was pointless to go on defending themselves and would admit their responsibility and offer us a reasonable settlement. I thought it would be such a relief not to have to drag this thing out any longer.

At home that night we all had a feeling of intense anticipation. I was virtually praying that it could all be over soon. I had hardly eaten anything for two weeks and I had had very little sleep. Every evening had been the same. When we arrived home, although I was no longer physically in the courtroom, mentally I couldn't remove myself from it. I found myself reviewing every detail of what had gone on and trying to imagine how the jury was viewing it. The worst part was always at night when I got into bed alone. Although I was exhausted, sleep took its time coming. I would try to stop myself from thinking about the day's events, but the more I tried, the more I focused on the details—what the marketing researcher had said, how Mr. Willing had talked, the way Mr. Beatie questioned a witness. On and on my mind raced, reviewing and reliving, while the hours ticked away. I was physically and mentally tired, and I didn't think I could take too much more. I had also begun to worry about getting fired from my job—I had already been away from it for too long. But at least Mike would be here in the morning, I comforted myself, and with luck this business might be over soon.

Mike had been given such short notice to return to New York that he had taken the Red Eye Express, which meant that he was flying all night. We were beginning to get worried about all this coast-to-coast hopping, with me losing pay and the cost of plane fares, and this time Mike had taken a six-week leave of absence since we had decided that it was important for him to be present for all of the second trial. But it had to be done, and we would just have to worry about the consequences afterward, we decided.

The night flight wouldn't give Mike time to come up to West Nyack after he had arrived, so it was arranged that his parents would pick him up at the airport early in the morning and take him back to their house for a shower and a quick change. Then he would get to the courthouse just in time for the judge's charging of the jury.

Mike arrived on time and everything worked out exactly except that his parents had no hot water in their apartment that morning. Poor Mike looked miserable when he came into the courtroom. He was completely exhausted from flying through the entire night and hadn't even been able to have a refreshing shower. But I was certainly happy to see him.

We all sat silently as Justice Fraiman charged the jury and sent them off into the deliberation room. Waiting for the jury to return with its verdict was almost unbearable. Judge Finz had said that if they were gone for a short time, it was good for us, so as time went on we became increasingly anxious. We waited in the courtroom, we waited out of the courtroom, we marched around the hallways. We sat down, we stood up, we fidgeted. We all did a great deal of pacing. We were a larger group that day because not only had Mike come, but Dennis and Felice as well. Gradually, we all

117

became disheartened while Mr. Beatie and his entourage gained in confidence.

After waiting for two hours I had started to feel nauseous from worry. Why are they taking so long? I kept asking myself, it's such a simple question to answer. But on and on we waited.

Suddenly, Charlie the court clerk announced that the jurors were coming back in. They had decided. We hurried to take our places in the courtroom. My throat felt tight from nervousness. I held on to the hands of my mother and husband. I had never been so tense before—my limbs were virtually rigid. This was so important to me. It was important because I knew we were right.

The six jurors marched in. Their expressions were somber as they took their places in the jury box. They didn't look at me—except for juror number six, a pleasant-faced middle-aged woman who had seemed to follow all the testimonies very carefully. As she came in she looked at us and shook her head slowly. No, she seemed to be saying; she looked so sad. My heart pounded heavily in my chest. Juror number six had just told us that the verdict was against us. It was against us! How? We had all seen number six. I clutched Mom's and Mike's hands.

Justice Fraiman asked the jury foreman to stand. "Was the DES that Mrs. Bichler took manufactured by Eli Lilly & Co.? What does the jury find?" he asked.

The foreman, a middle-aged gentleman who had dozed through much of the trial, looked up at the judge. "Yes," he said.

Mike and I stared at each other. "Yes"? That meant the jury had found in our favor. "Yes" meant that they believed Lilly *had* made the DES. "Yes" meant that we had read number six wrong. *We had won!*

My father stood up. We all started to rise, shaking our heads in bewilderment, with smiles on our faces.

Judge Finz, Sybil, and Ed turned around to us, also smiling. My heart was thumping, but from joy now. I was grinning from ear to ear. But then, within a split second, Fraiman was pounding on his desk, calling for everyone to quiet down. I looked at the jury box, where the other five jurors looked upset. They were muttering to the foreman. The foreman stared at the others for a second and then obviously realized his mistake. "Oh," he said, "I meant to say 'No.' "

My heart seemed to thump in my throat. There was a murmur throughout the courtroom. What? I couldn't believe it. I couldn't believe they could be so mean. They had to be wrong. Justice Fraiman was furious. He called for silence again and questioned the foreman. The foreman looked extremely embarrassed as he confirmed that the verdict was, in fact, "No"; the jury could not say that Lilly had manufactured the DES my mother had taken.

Justice Fraiman asked each juror to respond individually. All of them said "No," except for number six, who said "Yes." She seemed ready to hold onto that answer forever. In a civil case in New York only five out of six jurors had to agree to reach a verdict. And after all their deliberations there were five people who said "No." We had lost.

The jurors were dismissed. I sat staring at the floor. I held Mike's hand tight. I had made the decision not to cry. Lilly had made me cry seven years ago, when I had had cancer. No matter what, I was not going to cry now. I felt hardened. Judge Finz shook Beatie's hand. I wanted to puke. Beatie was just glowing and strutting. I couldn't blame him, but I also couldn't bear to look at him. As I rose from my seat, I caught a glimpse of Beatie's girlfriend, who had come every day to the court. She was looking at me with pity in her eyes. I didn't want that. I hated that look.

I left the courtroom. We all stood in the hallway.

Everyone was shaken. Judge Finz kept saying that he couldn't believe the verdict. He had been sure we'd won. He said that nine out of ten juries would have brought back a verdict in our favor.

"What use is that to us?" I demanded angrily. "We got the tenth jury and we lost. And that's that. It's over."

"We mustn't despair," continued Judge Finz. "We lost the battle but we can still win the war."

I glared at him. During all those weeks before the trial, everyone had said how important it was to win the first trial, to establish that Lilly was the manufacturer of my mother's DES. Although we still had the joint enterprise liability theory for the next trial, it had never been tested before and we had no guarantees that it would be accepted now. And here was Judge Finz now saying we could do it. Bull! How could I go on? I suddenly felt hopeless. It was all so expensive; I was losing all those wages and might possibly lose my job and Mike's job, too, in the process. A wave of desperation made me shudder. It was too trying for me; I had already lost a great deal of weight because I wasn't eating. Much worse was what the trial and this verdict were doing to my parents. Mom was upset and Dad looked really sick. They couldn't take this loss— they knew how important it was for me. They knew how much it hurt me and it hurt them double.

Judge Finz was still talking, but I couldn't hear him. Mike put his arm around me to comfort me, but I couldn't deal with that, and I drew away. All I could focus on was the pain in my parents' faces.

I suddenly felt I had to be on my own. I walked over to the window that overlooked an inner courtyard. It looked out across to the windows on the other side of the building. It was a dismal view but the outside air was refreshing and it felt good to be away from every-one.

I felt that the system had let me down. I had been skeptical about the system to begin with but I hadn't wanted to be. I had wanted to be shown that it would work. I felt small and very hurt. We were fighting a multibillion-dollar industry, I thought bitterly, and how naive I had been to think that we had even had a chance—despite the fact that we were right. I was glad that we had at least put up a fight, but I wasn't prepared to put myself or my family through any more of this, especially when it would obviously be an uphill battle. I might be a fighter, I thought, but I'm not a masochist. It was over.

Sybil came over to comfort me and to let me know that my drawing away was upsetting everyone else. I really had come to like Sybil and trusted her. I appreciated that she was concerned about my family. I rejoined the group, though I didn't think it was fair that once again I had to hide my feelings so others wouldn't be upset.

I told Judge Finz that I had decided not to pursue the second trial, which was scheduled to start on Monday, in four days' time. I was quite adamant about it, and Finz said that it was my choice but that I should think about it some more before giving him a final decision. I agreed to call him the next day.

That night, Mike and I held each other a lot. We spent most of the night talking. We talked about a lot of things. We talked about the trial and the pain we had endured. Mike didn't say anything to me directly, but I suppose he gently got me to admit that I wasn't ready to walk away from the issue just yet. I wasn't ready for defeat, despite my disappointment that day.

As we lay in each other's arms, I gradually felt the old anger rising in me. Anger and rage that gave me strength again. We talked more. Just because Eli Lilly & Co. was bigger, stronger, and more powerful than we were, we reasoned, and had lots of money, there was no reason why they should be able to walk away from the DES issue without being held in the slightest degree accountable and responsible for what they had done to so many people in this country. I knew I couldn't just walk away from the issue feeling beaten. I had survived the pain of cancer, and now I saw that I had survived the decision of the jury today. I did have the strength to go through with trial number two. As long as I had that strength, I would fight Lilly. They were wrong and I wasn't really ready to give up and roll over dead.

There was more to it than that, of course. We knew that the public was interested in the DES issue—the *New York Post* article was evidence of that. If nothing else, win or lose, we had an invaluable opportunity to let the American public know that the pharmaceutical companies placed a drug on the market that was a known cancer causer in animals. This was known as early as 1939, yet the drug (DES) was given to millions of pregnant women. The public had to know—had to be aware that this had happened and could happen again. Walking away from it all now would be giving up that opportunity, and, in many ways, evading the responsibility we had toward all the other people affected by DES as well as all consumers in this country. I knew that one of the big tragedies of the DES issue was that there were many people who still didn't know that they had been exposed to DES, who were walking around, just as I had done, without knowing that their bodies had been affected by this terrible drug. They needed to "ask their mothers," they needed to get special examinations, they needed to be aware of what had been done to them. If nothing else came out of this trial, if I didn't get compensated for what had happened to me, at least I could be in a position to alert others, to urge them to get the help they needed before it was too late. I could at least let the public know that tragedies such as this do happen, so that we can make sure they don't happen again.

That night I was transformed from someone who felt very small and timid, and too shy to talk much about what had happened—someone who had accepted only with uncertainty a duty to help other DES daughters—into another person—someone who no longer had just her own individual concern. I saw that I really did represent an issue. This case was an important one for every American consumer. While the DES issue was my issue, I owed it to others to make the most of it.

Before I fell asleep, I decided that the next morning I would speak to Mom and Dad. If they felt they couldn't go on, then it would be over. I couldn't force them to go through this again if they didn't want to. But if they were willing, I would be ready to call up Judge Finz and let him know we were still in it.

In the morning I got up with renewed determination. Mom and Dad were already downstairs having breakfast. They looked up at me to see how upset I still was. I sat down and asked them what they thought about going on with the second trial. They looked completely surprised. The night before I had gone to bed firm in my belief that it was all over. Mom did look hesitant but said nothing at first. Dad looked at me directly in the eye and said we should continue. He was positive we would win in the end. Then Mom said that I should do what I want. She was concerned about what the toll would be on me—she had seen how I had suffered through the first trial—but she didn't mind continuing, she said; she was a fighter too. However, she said that if we did continue, I had to promise to eat more. I hugged her hard, and promised.

I called up Judge Finz. He said that Sybil and Ed were with him in his office at that moment. They had been discussing the next part of the trial. I told him how I felt. "I want to continue," I said.

"I never doubted that you would, Joyce," Finz replied.

"Oh," I said. I was quite taken aback. But at the same time I was pleased. We were all fighters.

Judge Finz then proceeded to give me a rousing pep talk about how we could do it, how we would really show them, how we were in the right, and how truth and justice always won. It was effective and I felt good. I could feel his genuine concern and involvement in this. It was important to him as much as to me. But this time I was determined not to count on anything and not to go into this trial because I thought we were going to win. I hoped we would win, but this trial would also serve other purposes. Win or lose, we were going to take on Eli Lilly & Co., in effect the entire pharmaceutical industry, and fight them for as long as we could.

CHAPTER 11

It was Monday, June 4, 1979. The first day of trial number two. We were in the same courtroom, sitting in our regular places. We sat through the selection of the jury once again. This time the selection process was much more detailed and much slower. The potential jurors were questioned about their own health histories, those of their families, and their feelings about cancer. The process went on and on. One woman was excused on the grounds that she had a DES daughter. As she left the jury box, she walked past our row and wished us luck. That made me feel good.

The jury selection went on for two days. At last it was over; we had our jury. The foreman was a large, middle-aged black man, a businessman. Juror number two was a middle-aged black woman, a nurse. Number three was a young black woman who had a young child and worked in a nursery school. Number four was a young black man, a bank teller. Number five was a middle-aged white man who worked in the post office. And number six was a middle-aged white woman whose daughter was a nurse. Two alternates were also chosen.

This was our jury. I was going to get to know all of them well—not by speaking with them but by watching every expression on their faces, every movement of their eyes and by being with them in that courtroom every day from 10:00 A.M. to 5:00 P.M.

Although I was cautious, I felt good about these jurors. They seemed alert and intelligent. They seemed to take their roles seriously, which I liked. They would be the people to control my fate—much more so than the previous jury. But I didn't feel as trusting as I had during the first trial. I felt I no longer had any control over what was to happen. The show was under way again.

I realized that I was going to need a lot more moral support for this trial than I had originally thought. During the first trial I had asked friends and relatives not to come to the courthouse. I felt it was embarrassing to be displayed in such a setting and for some reason, I thought that it would be less of a trauma if I could isolate myself from others as much as possible. But after that first trial, I saw that isolation only made it harder. I did need others around me. I needed it, we all needed it. Our little group sat on the right-hand side of the courtroom. We barely took up one row. On the left-hand side, across the aisle, sat an enormous number of lawyers and clerks who represented not only Lilly but the other big drug companies as well. It wasn't just Lilly who was concerned about the outcome of this case. They all certainly had their representation. Well-dressed attorneys frequently came in to sit for a few hours listening to the proceedings and then went back and billed the drug company they were representing, in preparation for some future DES case. There was a striking difference between the two sides of the courtroom.

A lot of people stared at us and I always felt uncomfortable but I also stared back defiantly. I kept wondering how they could justify what they were doing —particularly the young women who worked for those firms. Didn't they realize that they could have been sitting here instead of me? Didn't they realize that whatever good the pharmaceutical companies did, they were also major culprits in endangering women's health? Didn't these women know they were working against their sisters?

I needed more support, and since I was now prepared to fight a political battle, I decided I ought to contact DES Action in New York. DES Action is a consumer group dedicated to giving support to the DES-exposed (mothers, daughters, and sons) as well as disseminating information about DES to the public and to health professionals, so that people would become aware of possibly having been exposed to DES. I had known for some time that DES groups existed, and had known Sybil had been in touch with them prior to this trial, but I had never been able to bring myself to contact one. I had been afraid. Until I had become able to talk about my own DES exposure, I was loath to contact such a group. But I was ready now. The trial put me in the position of having to face the fact that I was DES-exposed and that I had had a hysterectomy and a vaginectomy (a word I could never say before) because of it. I needed help now, and DES Action seemed like the place to turn for it.

I called and spoke to the national president, Fran Fishbane, herself a DES mother. The response was enthusiastic support. "We knew there was a trial about to go on. Why didn't you call us sooner?" My excuses were accepted; she understood how I had felt and was delighted that I had finally called them.

The New York DES Action group was located at Long Island Jewish Hospital in New Hyde Park, quite a long distance away from the Bronx, but they were able to mobilize their forces and before I knew it I had the names and phone numbers of several DES daughters who lived in the surrounding neighborhood. From then on, after spending long, tiring days in court I spent long, tiring evenings on the phone. Either I called them, or they called me. Throughout the day women and men I had never met before would take time off from their jobs and drop in to the courtroom to show their support and give me encouragement. All of them had either been affected by DES themselves or had someone close to them who had. They were grateful to me; they felt they were getting satisfaction by having someone stand up and fight the drug companies who were responsible.

Many of these women had tried to sue the drug companies themselves, but, as usual, because of the statute of limitations, or because it was so difficult to pinpoint a specific manufacturer, they had not been able to get their cases to court. Some women had their cases pending and were watching mine very closely, while others would have a chance if we won because even those who could not prove which drug company had manufactured their DES would then have a legal basis for bringing suit.

I gained so much from these contacts. For the first time I had the chance to speak to other DES daughters, other women who knew what it was like to be constantly concerned about the private parts of one's body, others who really knew what it felt like to worry about the cancer coming back at any moment. Or those who had to be aware of the possible effects of DES—not cancer, in their case, but who nonetheless had to live with the worry of having been exposed to a potential timebomb.

The first time I spoke to someone else who also had had the adenocarcinoma that I had gotten from DES I experienced such a strong feeling of sisterhood, of kinship. Here was another person who knew what it was like to have a uterus and vagina torn out of her body at a young age. We compared experiences, and how uncannily similar we found they were. I found it comforting to be able to talk about things that I had thought were unique to me since the surgery. For instance, I had always felt embarrassed talking about my bladder problems and the length of time it had taken before any sensation returned in the area. I had believed that I was the only one who had ever had to deal with such a problem, but now I was discovering that it was a common experience for any DES daughter who had had surgery similar to mine. Before, I had felt very sorry for myself, and bitter about all I had had to endure and the fact that it had happened to me at all. Talking to others who had gone through it didn't change those feelings, but it did help to make me feel much less alone, less different.

I spoke to many women who had had the same kind of cancer and the same kind of surgery. I realized that many of them had suffered more than I had—many had complications as well as recurrent disease. I heard stories about DES daughters who hadn't made it, women who had died because the cancer had not been caught in time. In many ways such tales served to heighten my fears, but at least such fears were more soundly brought to the surface, where they could be dealt with, rather than repressed. It was better to acknowledge what realistically could happen rather than let one's mind wander, fearing everything. For years, every time I had had an ache or a pain, deep down inside a voice would come up and ask if this was a recurrence of cancer somewhere in my body. Another voice would answer and say, No, don't be ridiculous. But the fear haunted me constantly. Each year of survival would bring more thanks to my lips and some sense of ease, but every time I made an appointment with the doctor for my six-months' check-up, the tension would build weeks before and not subside until all the reports had come back clear. And for all of us, the hardest thing to deal with was the fact that no one knew what the future would bring. The oldest DES daughter was now only in her mid-thirties, and most were only in their twenties. No one could predict anything, but fears about other cancers resulting from exposure to DES are not unrealistic.

It did help to talk; I realized I was luckier than many; I was a survivor. It gave me great encouragement to talk to women who had had surgery before I had, to know that they were still around. But it was also good to be able to talk to someone who had only recently had their surgery and have them be encouraged by the fact that I was seven years postsurgical, and doing fine.

I gained so much when I contacted DES Action—not just the support I had needed. By talking to all these women I had taken another step in the healing process. I realized then that the healing was still going on, even seven years after the operation.

Four women in particular became very important to me during the trial because of the support they gave. Linda and Margo were both DES daughters themselves and although they did not have the cancer associated with the drug, they did have a more common problem —cell changes in the vagina and cervix—that also results from DES exposure. They had suffered a lot; they had had minor surgery and had to live with the constant fear of cancer appearing. They came to the trial whenever they could. Naomi and Chris were not DES daughters, but were friends of Linda and so indirectly knew what it was like to be DES-exposed. All four of them were wonderful. Even though they had been strangers to me before, they were as important to me throughout the trial as the rest of my legal team. They were just what I needed for support.

The opening statements for this trial lasted much longer than for the first. Again they gave only the framework of the case for both sides. As before, Judge Finz made his statement first. He said that our case would show that the pharmaceutical companies had pooled their research in the 1940s in order to get DES approved by the FDA and that Eli Lilly had been the leader of this scheme. Judge Finz said that we would show that despite this pooling of research, DES had not been tested properly before it was put out on the market. Furthermore, he said, there was evidence at the time that DES caused cancer; eighteen years after my mother had taken it, it caused my cancer. Therefore, according to the joint enterprise liability theory, all those drug companies were guilty of doing inadequate research on DES before marketing the drug. Eli Lilly, as one of these drug companies, was as responsible as any of them for damages arising from use of DES, and Lilly as the major manufacturer of DES was liable for compensating me.

Next it was Mr. Beatie's turn. He stated that they would show that DES had been properly tested, and that had it not been for this drug, I would never have been born. He also said that their case would show that my cancer was not caused by DES at all, but by other factors.

Both Finz and Beatie said a lot more, but all the important details were going to come out over the course of the trial. Although there was already much technical medical jargon being used, the jury looked alert and comprehending and ready to listen intently to all that was said.

Our first witness was Dr. Alan Goldman, a renowned teratologist from the Children's Hospital at the University of Pennsylvania Medical School. Teratology is the study of malformations in otherwise normal organisms. In this case, Dr. Goldman was reporting on drugs that caused malformations in the fetus. Dr. Goldman had the typical appearance of a man dedicated to his research. He was small and thin, with disheveled hair and a wrinkled suit. He kept producing his important papers from an ordinary old shopping bag.

Dr. Goldman was a leading expert in teratology and, as happened with all the expert witnesses, when he first took the stand much time was spent establishing to the jury that he was indeed an expert. Judge Finz questioned him about every article he had ever published and the reputation of every journal in which his name had ever appeared, and every award and piece of critical acclaim he had won. Once it was established that Goldman was indeed an expert in his field, Judge Finz could concentrate on his testimony.

I learned a great deal from Dr. Goldman's testimony.

It was extremely interesting and very important. One of our arguments was that the drug companies (including Eli Lilly) did not do adequate research into DES during the 1940s, that they never did proper animal testing on the drug before giving it to pregnant women. For this argument to stand up, we had to show that animal testing was used during the 1940s, when DES was being tested. Obviously, if animal testing was not used at that time, the drug companies could not be held responsible for testing this drug on animals.

Dr. Goldman gave strong testimony to show that animal testing certainly was done throughout the 1940s. He used his own research papers and quoted several 1940 studies to back up his statement.

Next, Judge Finz asked Dr. Goldman to discuss studies that showed that there were certain drugs, which, when taken by pregnant females, passed through the placental barrier and caused harmful effects in the offspring. In particular, Dr. Goldman mentioned a drug that when given to a pregnant mouse caused lung cancer in its babies. This effect had been acknowledged and noted in medical journals even before the testing of DES. Thus Dr. Goldman established the fact that the pharmaceutical companies should have known that there were drugs that could cross the placenta and adversely affect the fetus. These drugs are called teratogens.

Dr. Goldman's next point was that early animal studies on DES in the late 1930s and early 1940s showed that it was a teratogen. They showed that the offspring of females exposed to DES while pregnant had visible mutations—mainly involving their sexual organs. In addition, other early studies showed that animals directly exposed to DES developed cancer. In fact, Dr. Goldman said, some medical journals in the 1940s warned people in their editorial columns to beware of DES because it possibly did have the potential to cause cancer.

With this information, Judge Finz asked Dr. Goldman, where did things go wrong? How did the drug get on the market?

Dr. Goldman continued. After these critical tests, he said, the drug companies soon got hold of DES and started their own research. The drug had tremendous potential because it was the first synthetic estrogen. Estrogens are female sex hormones and were prescribed whenever doctors felt a woman had a problem producing her own estrogen. But natural estrogens were expensive and in short supply. In 1938, Sir Charles Dodds in England developed a method of producing the first synthetic estrogen—diethylstilbestrol (DES). This was hailed as a major breakthrough, for now oral estrogens could be manufactured cheaply and in large quantities.

That day's testimony revealed a lot to me about the history of DES. Sir Charles did not patent his brainchild but instead gave it as a gift to the world. The gift was quickly snatched up by the drug companies, which were going to put this "miracle drug" to many uses. DES was to be used to inhibit lactation in women who did not want to breast-feed their babies; on men who had prostate cancer; and on postmenopausal women as an estrogen replacement.

In 1941, DES was approved by the Food and Drug Administration (FDA) for these uses, but the pharmaceutical companies wanted to use DES on pregnant women. It was believed that women who had a tendency to miscarry would benefit from extra doses of this synthetic estrogen. Diabetic women tended to have problems in pregnancy, and it was thought that DES would help there, too. The excitement over this drug was enormous. DES was hailed as the wonder drug, and one researcher even went so far as to say that DES would make a normal pregnancy even more normal! So the drug companies were going to test DES on pregnant women.

Against this background, Dr. Goldman went on to explain to the court the differences between controlled and noncontrolled research studies. A controlled study is one in which there are two groups being tested. Both groups are as alike as possible, and conditions are exactly the same in both groups. The only difference is that one group is given the drug being tested, while the other group is given a placebo, or sugar pill. Therefore, if there is any significant variance in the results between the two groups, it can be attributed only to the drug. An even better study is a double-blind controlled study. This is when even the people who are administering the medications do not know which group is receiving the real drug, and which the placebo. Of course, the people receiving the pills also do not know which they are getting. This double-blind method eliminates any biased treatment or psychological effects that may influence a study.

Dr. Goldman explained that controlled studies were common even back in the 1940s. These methods were well known, and responsible researchers put them to use. He then stated that Eli Lilly and other drug companies had *not* used controlled studies between 1941 and 1947, when they were testing DES on pregnant women. All they had used were "historical studies," in which the researchers had looked at the histories of past pregnancies during which DES had not been given, and then they had compared those with the results in the same women when they were pregnant again and DES *was* given. The problem with such studies, Dr. Goldman told the court, is that if a difference between the results is shown, there is no way of knowing to what to attribute it. For instance, a woman may be less likely to miscarry simply because, being in a study, she gets better medical attention. Or, because she miscarried previously, she may just be more careful about doing things during the next pregnancy. Or it is possible that some women who do miscarry will eventually carry through with a normal pregnancy, anyway. Whatever the case, the fact is that with a historical study there is no way anyone can say that success is a result of having taken the drug. And, when they were testing DES, the pharmaceutical companies had used no control studies at all.

Guided on by Judge Finz, Dr. Goldman pointed out that DES had never been tested on pregnant animals before being given to pregnant women. He said he had always been astonished by this fact, particularly since if tests *had* been done on pregnant mice, the six-month-old female offspring (the equivalent, he said, to a twenty-year-old human) would show cancer of the cervix and vagina. Such a study had been done years later and had shown exactly this.

The technology of animal testing was well-known and in particular the technology to perform tests on mice for carcinogenic effect was known. This was standard research science as it existed in 1947. The drug companies had to be aware of DES's lack of efficacy before my mother took the drug.

As Dr. Goldman explained all this, I found myself clenching my fists with rage. I had known that the drug companies had done incompetent research, but I hadn't realized that they had been quite as irresponsible as this respected doctor was saying. They hadn't bothered to do a simple and necessary test that would have prevented all the pain and suffering that I and others had had to endure. They had just used pregnant women as the guinea pigs, in completely unreliable tests.

In 1947, the FDA approved the use of DES on pregnant women. Its approval was based on the research done by the drug companies. Dr. Goldman testified that five years later, Dr. William J. Dieckmann of the University of Chicago and Chicago Lying-In Hospital conducted a properly controlled study on the effect of DES on pregnant women (using Eli Lilly DES pills). Dr. Dieckmann did not believe that any of the previous re-

search on the drug had been scientifically accurate. The
study was completed in 1952 and the results reported
in a prestigious medical journal: They concluded that
DES was not effective in preventing miscarriages. However, despite the Dieckmann Chicago study (published
before Mom was prescribed DES) as well as other
studies confirming his findings, the pharmaceutical companies did not take the drug off the market. DES was
prescribed for pregnant women for the next twenty
years. DES was not banned for use in pregnancy until
1971.

An important concept that Dr. Goldman introduced
during his testimony was the "risk : benefit ratio." This
is a major concept in almost any medical issue and was
constantly mentioned in our trial. The value of a new
drug, Dr. Goldman explained, is decided by weighing
the harm it might do (risks) against the benefits it
might bring. If the benefits outweigh the risks, then it is
obviously a drug worth using. In each situation, the
risk : benefit ratio may change but it must always be
considered. Back in 1953, when DES was given to my
mother, it was known that the risks associated with
DES were high. It was known that it was a teratogen,
that it could cross the placenta and affect the fetus,
and that it had a cancer potential. With the publication of the Dieckmann study in 1953, it was also
known that DES did not, in fact, prevent miscarriages.
It did not do what was claimed for it. Therefore, in
1953 it became clear that the risks were high and the
benefit was zero. Yet Eli Lilly & Co. kept making this
drug and recommending it for use on pregnant women.

Dr. Goldman testified for three whole days. What he
had to say was appalling, fascinating, and terrifying all
at the same time. Every point he made was strongly
backed up by published medical articles. The more I
learned, the angrier I became. The story of DES was
more horrifying and disgraceful than I could ever have

imagined. Surely, I thought, the jury will feel the same. And how could Eli Lilly defend themselves in the light of all of Dr. Goldman's information? I had gotten cancer because the only thing the drug companies had cared about was profits.

Another important witness for us was a man who wasn't even there in court. Dr. Hines was a very elderly gentleman who lived in California. He had been the chief researcher for Eli Lilly & Co. back in the 1940s. Mr. Beatie had taken Dr. Hines' lengthy deposition a few years earlier. He had been too frail even then to come to court and testify in person, so that Mr. Beatie had obtained court permission to videotape his testimony. Apparently there were twelve hours of these tapes. He was a witness for the defense and the thought of listening to a distinguished old doctor talk about the virtues of Eli Lilly & Co. was not very appealing. However, Judge Finz knew that there were some important things Dr. Hines had to say that would help our case. Instead of waiting for Mr. Beatie to show the tapes, or showing them himself, Judge Finz decided to read parts of the transcript to the court. He could pick out relevant points without putting everyone through all those hours of tape. Judge Finz, Sybil, and Mr. Julien had spent long hours in the past reviewing these tapes.

Dr. Hines' testimony was central to the issue of joint enterprise liability in this case. He had been the top researcher at Lilly and had worked to get FDA approval for the marketing of DES. In his testimony, Dr. Hines stated that Lilly's first application to the FDA was turned down, on the ground that the testing up to then had not been adequate enough to warrant FDA approval. At that same time in the 1940s, there were several other major pharmaceutical companies working to get DES approved, including Abbott Laboratories and E. R. Squibb. Dr. Hines got in contact with the top researchers at the other companies and they decided

DES DAUGHTER

that instead of working independently on their research to improve their FDA applications for DES, they would form a joint committee to pool their information, thus making it easier to get approval.

Dr. Hines stated that a "small" committee was thus formed and he, as a Lilly representative, became the head of that committee. The companies shared the results of their respective research, but filed independent applications with the FDA. And finally, the FDA approved the use of DES.

Dr. Hines' testimony established that the pharmaceutical companies had not been working independently or in competition with one another. It had been more beneficial to them to pool their resources and act as a joint force to get a profitable drug approved by the FDA. Information had been shared between them, not hidden; they had acted in concert to get DES approved. This fact was crucial to our case. Even though we hadn't been able to prove that Eli Lilly was the actual manufacturer of my mother's DES, it didn't matter. Dr. Hines' testimony revealed that all the major pharmaceutical companies were responsible for the inadequate testing of the drug. And Lilly, as the head of the drug companies' joint research committee, could certainly be held responsible for damages caused by the drug.

Another interesting point that Judge Finz selected from the transcript of Dr. Hines' testimony was that Hines had indeed been aware that DES had a cancer potential, but, Hines said, since the rates of cancer were not "significant," they continued to work to get FDA approval anyway.

Although Judge Finz was masterful at picking out the important passages from the reams of paper, he did have to read quite a bit of the testimony before and after each point in order to show that it was in context. The readings went on for hours. I was quite impressed that the jurors really tried to follow each word closely.

That's not to say that at times a few jurors didn't doze off, but at least some of them were always listening intently at any one time. And it wasn't just the jurors who were put to sleep by these readings; my poor mother, who was having difficulty sleeping at night, often started to nod out next to me. It wasn't that the testimony wasn't interesting, it was just that she was exhausted. I was sympathetic to her weariness, but I didn't think the jurors should see her sleeping through her own trial. So every time her eyes closed I discreetly poked her with my elbow so that she would wake up. Watching out for Mom gave me something to do so that I wouldn't fall asleep myself. In fact, it became pretty comic because, I discovered, Dad was also trying to stop Mom falling asleep. Every time she closed her eyes for a second, my father and I would poke her on each side to keep her awake. And poor Mom would open her eyes again with a start.

I found that I was learning not only more about DES but also about the operations of the pharmaceutical companies. In my naïveté, I had believed that the drug companies were humanitarian institutions. I had really believed that. Gradually I was realizing that the pharmaceutical industry is made up of large corporations and, like any large corporation, they are in business to make money. Profit is their ultimate goal. The fact that their business happens to be in the field of human health is virtually irrelevant. Of course it can still be argued that they do good; many of their products have certainly helped people. But Eli Lilly isn't in business for the good of the people; it is in business to make money. Its choices are made with that aim in mind. Until I realized all this, I couldn't understand how Lilly could put a drug like DES on the market. From a consumer standpoint it is an incomprehensible action. But from a corporate standpoint it is perfectly understandable. The pharmaceutical companies don't work toward consumer goals, they work toward corporate goals. My eyes were opened, and I was a lot less naive than I had been before. I saw that Eli Lilly was not going to represent consumer interests, and I saw that it is up to consumers to stand up and represent themselves, and fight for their interests.

CHAPTER 12

What about the role of the Food and Drug Administration in all this? As a government watchdog, wasn't the FDA ultimately responsible for allowing DES on the market? Sybil, during the pre-trial preparations, had subpoenaed our next witness and I was anxious to hear him. Dr. Theodore G. Klumpp, who had been chief of the Drug Division of the FDA at the time DES was approved. He was the person who had been instrumental in getting DES on the market. He was not a very cooperative witness. For one thing, he had claimed that he was too ill to come to court, even though when he was served with the subpoena he was apparently up a ladder painting his house. Justice Fraiman had ordered a court-appointed doctor to examine him, and after a delay of several days it was determined that he was healthy enough to come to court. When he finally took the witness stand he was very hostile to Judge Finz.

His testimony opened my eyes even further. I had always viewed the FDA as an independent agency that monitored, amongst other things, the pharmaceutical industry. Was I ever wrong! The ties between that industry and the FDA are almost as close as those between the drug companies themselves. Dr. Klumpp testified that during the 1940s the FDA did *no* independent testing of its own on drugs submitted for its approval. That it had no laboratories, and no researchers for testing whether a drug was safe or effective. It only had facilities to test whether a drug was indeed made up of the compounds that the companies claimed it was—for instance, whether DES was actually made up of diethylstilbestrol. The FDA based its decisions on the research carried out by the drug companies themselves. The pharmaceutical companies paid for the research and then submitted for FDA approval only those results they thought were important. At that time, the FDA simply set down the very minimum of standards, and all research submitted to them had to show that it met that minimum. Lilly's first application for approval of DES was rejected by the FDA in 1939. The drug company had insufficient information to warrant approval at that time. There was still concern about the drug's cancer potential. But there seemed to be inside pressure to get it approved, and Dr. Klumpp was the person who actually pushed for FDA approval of DES.

Before Dr. Klumpp left the stand, Judge Finz asked him what his salary had been while he worked for the FDA. Dr. Klumpp replied that he had earned approximately $6,000 per year—a nice salary during that time. Finz then asked him what he had earned the following year, after he had left the FDA. Dr. Klumpp shifted uncomfortably in his seat. He said that he had left the FDA to become president of Winthrop Laboratories (one of the drug companies filing for DES approval). As president of Winthrop Laboratories, Dr. Klumpp had earned $30,000 per year. I later learned that almost every FDA commissioner during that time went from their FDA position to head one of the major pharmaceutical companies. As consumers we came out on the bottom again.

Our next witness was a wonderful man. Dr. Burton Krumholz worked at one of the New York State DES screening clinics set up in 1979 to provide services for DES-exposed women. He had been involved in DES research and has been seeing the DES-exposed for many years. Dr. Krumholz's testimony struck at the heart of the issue. He described the relationship between DES and cancer, and told the court how my type of cancer, adenocarcinoma of the vagina and cervix, had never been seen in young women under the age of thirty-five before the advent of DES use. He described the important studies done by Dr. Arthur Herbst of Massachusetts General Hospital, who first reported the connection between DES and adenocarcinoma of the vagina and cervix in 1971. Dr. Krumholz spoke of his own experiences seeing and treating women who have had this kind of cancer and had been exposed to DES, and he said he had examined my own medical records and that in his opinion my cancer had been caused by my mother's use of DES.

Dr. Krumholz came across as sincere and truthful. He was very knowledgeable and his manner down-to-earth. I got the impression that his testimony really had an effect on the jury.

Although Mr. Beatie tried to question his credibility during the cross-examination, Dr. Krumholz stood firm and repeated all that he knew about DES. I really had faith in him; he was someone who really cared about the entire DES issue.

Before the trial had begun, I had had to go for a thorough medical examination so that the report on my condition would be up-to-date. Dr. Daniel had retired some years before and anyway was unavailable, since he had moved to another state. So I had gone to see Dr. Charlton, who was still in practice in the Bronx. I had gone over to his office one afternoon, and was happy to see him again. Dr. Charlton seemed hesitant about getting involved in a legal case, but he also felt that there was much wrongdoing here, and he was willing to do what he could.

On the day Dr. Charlton was coming to court to testify, I was extremely nervous. The evidence was now to shift from general discussions about DES to specific points about me and what had happened in my case. It's not often that you get to hear your physician talk in detail about your medical condition, not holding back on anything, and I was apprehensive.

My concern must have been very noticeable because before Dr. Charlton had been called, Judge Finz took me aside. He suggested that since Dr. Charlton was going to be rather graphic about my cancerous condition when he talked to the court, it would perhaps be better if I weren't there to listen to him. I resented the implication that I couldn't take it, as though I were a small child, but I was also relieved that Judge Finz was giving me a chance to be absent, so that I wouldn't be pained by what was said. But I still wasn't sure and I protested. I told him that I did want to stay.

Just as Judge Finz started to try to persuade me again, my mother came up to us and said she didn't feel like going through all the medical details again. She wasn't up to it, she said, but she didn't want to stand out in the hallway by herself. That left me with little choice, so I stopped causing a fuss and agreed to stay outside with Mom. However, before I left, I made Mike promise to tell me everything that Dr. Charlton had to say.

Mom was looking very tired, but out in the hallway there was nowhere we could sit and be comfortable. So we walked slowly around the halls for a while and then, when our feet ached from pacing the hard marble floors, we ducked into another courtroom where another trial was in progress. To our great surprise, there was my cousin Steven, who, as assistant D.A. in the Bronx, was in the middle of trying a rape case. We sat down on a bench at the back and followed the trial for a time. There's nothing like listening to someone else's problems to take your mind off your own.

Dr. Charlton's testimony lasted for several hours. When Mom and I returned to the courtroom after it was over, everyone was saying that he was an effective witness and a wonderful, humanistic doctor. I knew that already. I didn't know, but found out later that he had spent much time reviewing the DES literature and had, even at his own expense, gone to see Dr. Arthur Herbst (the doctor who made the original DES and cancer connection) to discuss my individual situation with him. As I picked up my things, I glanced up at the blackboard that had been placed at the front of the courtroom. Various diagrams had been drawn on it, in white chalk, of my uterus and vagina and the cancer. There was one drawing depicting a large tumor overlapping the cervix and the vagina. It was up there on the blackboard, marked as evidence. Although I couldn't take my eyes off it, I didn't want it to be there. I couldn't wait to have Mike repeat to me what Dr. Charlton had said, yet I didn't really want to hear. I had seen it before, I had heard it before, and I had felt its effects before. I was glad to have missed Dr. Charlton's testimony; matters were tough enough as they were. I hadn't needed to hear him.

We had all been dreading the time when the family had to give testimony. It was hard enough for each of us to talk about our feelings to one another, let alone in front of a group of strangers. We all anticipated a total lack of privacy, total exposure. But the time had now come and we couldn't stop it.

Once again Dad was called to the stand first. This time Finz asked him to tell the court about me. Dad's voice was gentle as he described what sort of child I had been—happy and carefree even as a teenager. He said that I had changed dramatically after my illness. He hesitated as he began to describe his feelings about his baby girl being sick and having cancer. It was too private, I didn't want to listen. I could see tears glistening in Dad's eyes as he spoke. I shut my own eyes to fight back the tears that were flooding them. Dad went on to talk about Michael. He said he didn't know what would have happened to me had Michael not been there. I was clutching Mike's hand so hard his skin must have been pinched. I could hardly bear to listen as Dad started to describe the pain and hurt a parent experiences when a child is ill.

Dad's testimony went on for some time, but at last it was over. He came off the stand looking exhausted and worn. It was the end of the day, and we were able to go home. I couldn't talk to him about what he had said in his testimony. I did want to tell him that he shouldn't feel so hurt, that I was all right. But I couldn't say the words because I knew he was right to feel as he did. The cancer had happened, and I had changed, and the pain was still there. That day in court I had seen how much we all feel that pain. It wasn't just me.

In the middle of all the anguish about the trial and the upcoming testimony of the family, we had to stop and move into what seemed like another world. Andrew, my thirteen-year-old nephew, was being Bar Mitzvahed that weekend—my parents' first grandchild to become a man. It was a time of great joy.

If it had come at any other time, Mom would have been preparing for the Bar Mitzvah weeks in advance. She certainly would have been getting very excited. But these were not normal times. It was difficult for any of us to ignore the tension and pick up the happiness. And there was so much to do and prepare for—who had thought about dresses or matching shoes, or appointments to get one's hair done?

Saturday morning there was a flurry of activity from all of us. Everyone ran around doing all the things that should have been done days before. And in the end it was so good for us, for it did keep us busy and kept our minds off the trial. That alone was wonderful. And when we got to the synagogue and Andrew stood up tall and proud throughout the prescribed ritual, that was even more wonderful.

Joyce Bichler

The whole weekend was taken up by the Bar Mitzvah, as the celebration continued on to Sunday, when we had a reception for Andrew. It was a marvelous occasion, and the weekend did us all the world of good.

Monday came into our lives much too soon.

Although Mom had done so well on the stand during the first trial, she was still nervous about going through it again. She knew that this time it would be more grueling.

Once again she was called and sworn in. Once again she took the stand. Once again she described how and why she had been given those pills. She had to go through the history of all three of her pregnancies. She told the court that she had stained a little blood during the first three months of her pregnancies with Arlene and Dennis, but at that time her doctor had just advised her to stay in bed and rest. She had taken the doctor's advice and had had normal pregnancies and had delivered full-term babies. When she was pregnant with me, Mom said, the same symptoms appeared. She now had a new obstetrician (Dr. Fleischer), and he prescribed a drug for her "to help save the baby." She hadn't taken the drug for long, just a few weeks. As was her pattern, she had stopped bleeding after the third month. She had given birth to me at the right time in a normal delivery.

Mom then talked about my childhood in much the same way my father had. But when she mentioned my illness, she not only conveyed the sadness of that event but also the tremendous sense of guilt she carried with her, knowing that my disease had been caused by something she had taken. Mom's lips were trembling as she spoke. As I watched her I realized that tears were pouring down my cheeks. I knew how much Mom had suffered since I had been ill. We had talked about it in the past. She had taken the DES because she had wanted to have a baby and hadn't wanted to lose it. How could she not take a drug that the doctor told her was to

147

"help save the baby"? It must have been obvious to the jury that the drug had not just affected me but my mother as well.

When Mr. Beatie stood up to cross-examine Mom, I felt very angry at him. Couldn't he see that she was suffering enough? But he didn't seem to care. He questioned Mom about her pregnancy history and made her describe her symptoms in detail. He questioned her about the DES pills again—how many she had taken and how often. Then he sat down and left her alone.

There was a recess after my mother's testimony and when we resumed, Michael was called to the stand. There was Michael. I was embarrassed just seeing him there, for I knew what would be coming. I leaned up closer to my mother, who was back sitting next to me again.

Michael talked about meeting me, about school, about his job, and about when we got married. Judge Finz then questioned him about my illness and surgery. Michael talked about my state of mind immediately after and the reasons why he had stayed around. He said how much he loved me and how much it had hurt him to watch me suffer. He talked about our marriage, and how the surgery had affected it.

I could feel myself blushing as the questions and their answers began to be more intimate. I felt as though all eyes were on me. Mike was asked how our marriage was affected. He talked about my inability to have children. He said that that was an issue we were still dealing with, one that continued to upset me. He was asked about the vaginectomy, and then he was actually asked specific questions about our sex life. I was cringing. Judge Finz was handling the matter as delicately as possible and Michael was coping with it well. Those questioned tortured me, but I knew they had to be asked. Our sex life was a critical issue. After all, that was the core of what DES had done to me. One can fear cancer, one can be despondent about never being able to bear children, but those thoughts come and go. The change caused by having my vagina removed was something I had to face every night of my life. I managed to deal with it as well as I could, but the reminder was always there; I was never allowed to forget. I was always reminded that I was different. It doesn't go away.

Now here was Mike talking about these things. He was talking about sex in front of a room full of strangers. Worse yet, he was talking about it in front of my parents! Now he was crying. I was crying. It must have been so difficult for him to talk about what sex was like with his wife and to discuss his feelings about it. What a task. It was hard. He was upset, I was hysterical. I could no longer control myself. He was touching on the sore spot, the area that had never healed. Seven years' worth of pain came out in loud, uninhibited sobs. My mother turned to me and held me in her arms until it was over.

Tomorrow was my turn.

Since the first article about my case in the *New York Post*, there had been an enormous amount of publicity and increasing support from women's groups throughout the state. In the evenings I had been talking to women not only from DES Action but also from such organizations as Healthright, the National Women's Health Network, and the National Organization for Women (NOW). My case clearly had a political importance that was much greater than I had realized. It was not only a DES issue, it was also a broader feminist issue that directly concerned the well-being of all women. For the time being, I represented all the problems concerning women's health in general. In more ways than one, mine was a test case.

On the day I had to testify I knew that the support I had won would present itself in full force. I knew that this was the day when people would turn up en masse at the courthouse to be behind me and what I was doing. Many people had called to tell me that they would be there. They wanted to hear what I had to say; they wanted to show their concern. Many friends called to say that they would be taking time off from work that day, to be in court so that I wouldn't be alone. It scared me a little to think about talking on the stand with all these people listening, but it also made me feel good. I was overcome with a sense of purpose. The goal Mike and I had set out for at the beginning of this trial was becoming a reality. Inside, I knew that what I was doing was right. And we were making an impact. At the times when the hardship of the trial depressed me and my family, the support we received from others once again made it all meaningful and worthwhile. I shall be forever thankful to all those people who helped us continue with that trial. They gave us the reason to go on.

I was up early that morning. I had hardly slept at all the night before. I was scared enough of testifying, but I also felt a great sense of responsibility to all my friends and supporters who would be there that day. I would be telling my story. But it was my story only in part; it was really the story of all DES daughters.

I was shaking so much that I could hardly eat breakfast, but remembering my promise to my mother, I forced myself to eat what I could. It was a long drive to the Bronx. I began to feel panicked. To our delight and amazement when we finally arrived, outside the courthouse, on the steps, was an impressive demonstration. Women were gathering with DES posters and placards. They were all there to support me and to make a public statement about DES. It was wonderful. I was only sorry that I couldn't stay to watch or participate. I had to go into the courtroom and do my part.

I walked in and sat down. I just wanted to get it over with. Justice Fraiman came in and much time was spent discussing vital and complex legal matters. The discussions went on and on, and I felt increasingly tense.

At last it was time for me to go on the stand. I stood up and took the oath. As I sat down the doors to the courtroom started to swing open, and one by one people began to flow in. The demonstration outside had finished and now everyone was coming into the courtroom to show their support and listen to my testimony. One after another—women, men, strangers, friends, relatives—they all silently flowed in. They smiled at me, they gave me the victory sign, they were there. It was almost unbelievable, and it made me feel so good and so confident. And they kept coming. "Our" side of the courtroom was soon filled and the crowd overflowed onto Lilly's side, mingling with the lawyers from the different drug companies. Finally there were no more seats left and only standing room. I looked out over the crowd and saw close friends. I saw people I hadn't seen in years, people who had heard somehow through the grapevine that I needed support and had come down to give theirs. I saw women from DES Action and other groups. I saw reporters I recognized from the New York TV news stations. I saw reporters from the radio and newspapers, some of whom I had met during the course of the trial. I saw courtroom artists who were just starting their sketches. And there in the front, were Mom, Dad, Mike, Arlene, and Dennis. I suddenly felt quite detached from the scene. What was I, little Joyce Bichler of the Bronx, doing sitting here in this courtroom with all of these people looking at me? I didn't have much time to answer that. Judge Finz stood up and came over to me to start the questioning. I saw only him. Everyone else in the courtroom faded away. I took a deep breath. This was it.

I started out by giving the court basic background information about myself—my age, address, profession, and other factual details, which took up a fair bit of time. All this was helpful for me to get used to being on the stand. At one point Justice Fraiman gave me a fright when he told me rather harshly to speak up. I suppose I had been talking too softly. Judge Finz then slowly began to ask about more crucial points. I had to describe my original symptoms, my illness, and my hospital stay. Somehow all those facts seemed secondary at this moment because they had been raised so frequently by other witnesses during the trial. But then, I had to talk about how it all had affected me, not physically so much as emotionally.

I had difficulty finding the right words at first but gradually they came out more fluently as I felt the value of being able to speak out to all these people in front of me. I was glad to have the opportunity to speak out to the people who cared, but most of all I was speaking to Beatie and all the people who represented Eli Lilly & Co. I was speaking to the people who were responsible for my having cancer.

I told them about my nightmares, the awful dreams I had had long after my surgery. Nocturnal visions of being back in the hospital, visions of being riddled with disease, visions of being cut open again, visions of being chased by others and laid out on a stretcher.

As I spoke I felt that I was doing more than just telling my story. I was reliving much of it, and experiencing feelings I had never had before. The faces in front of me in that courtroom became clear to me again. I saw tenderness and care, concern and compassion all around. I saw interest, fascination, horror. And I saw eyes filling up with tears.

My voice suddenly became shaky again as I felt my emotions building up inside me. I pushed on. I told them how I felt about not being able to have children, and about my sense of inadequacy because of that. I told them my concerns about Michael and about how I felt guilty for not being able to make the choices that nearly every other woman can make. I felt guilty because I wasn't able to be a "normal" sexual partner. The more I talked, the more miserable I began to feel. I told them about how I felt like a freak, someone who was deformed because of DES and because of surgery. I repeated it. I *did* feel like a freak, and the circus of a court trial served to confirm that fact. I told them about my constant fear of cancer. I told them that every time I had an ache or a pain, I would immediately think, "This is it, I've got it again." I told them that I was always vulnerable, that I feared for my life and that that fear never totally left me.

I was conscious of forcing my words out through quivering lips as seven years of harbored rage emerged. I looked across at all those lawyers working for Lilly, defending a company that had caused so much pain and suffering. The anger I felt at that precise point was so intense it scared me. "It never should have happened, it never should have happened to me or to anyone else. It didn't have to happen. It never should have happened." My cheeks were burning as hot tears of bitterness poured down my face. And I broke down completely as I confessed that the reason I worked with the elderly was that I didn't think that I would ever get to be old myself.

It was over. I couldn't look up anymore. I couldn't move. I stayed in the witness box for a few minutes, gripping the sides of the chair. Judge Finz sat down. Mr. Beatie said he didn't wish to question me. Through my own weeping I could hear other people sobbing, other people in the courtroom crying for me.

It was my mother who came across to me and wiped my face. I hung on to her as we cried in each other's arms. I had done my best.

CHAPTER 13

I had been the last witness for our case, but the day was not over yet. Mr. Beatie was to start his case that afternoon after a long recess. During the recess I had a chance to meet many of the people who had come to the courtroom that day, but I was too exhausted to say much to them. However, I did tell them all how much I appreciated their presence in court.

The recess was over. We were back in our places. Although I felt I had virtually recovered from my ordeal that morning, my heart began to beat uncomfortably fast again.

Mr. Beatie started his fight quickly and heavily. The first person he called to the stand was my father. We were astonished. What could he want from Dad? My father took the stand again and was reminded that he was still under oath from having been sworn in the last time he had testified. Mr. Beatie started grilling him. He concentrated on Dad's medical history and kept raising the instances when my father had had cancer himself. My family had frequently been reassured by a number of doctors that my cancer had not been related to Dad's in any way. My cancer had been completely different from what my father had had. Whatever my genetic background was, the doctors had said: The cancer I had at the age of eighteen was definitely triggered by DES. But Mr. Beatie's inferences were clear. I was appalled. It was bad enough that my mother suffered from terrible feelings of guilt, and now this lawyer was trying to push the burden onto my father. What a low blow.

Dad looked very upset when he got off the stand.

Joyce Bichler

Although he knew that the point Beatie was trying to make was unfounded, he certainly hadn't expected his medical history to be examined and picked apart like that.

The day was at last over. As we drove back home in the car, we all felt battered by the day's events. We felt we were in the middle of a battle in which no one would be spared. I was afraid of what lay ahead, what plans Mr. Beatie had up his sleeve. We had already seen what kind of tricks he was prepared to use to defend Eli Lilly. I knew we all had to brace ourselves, but it was tough.

That night the TV news programs carried the story about the demonstration and the trial. The case was really heating up.

As was to be expected, Mr. Beatie was going to try to undermine all the points that we had made in our section of the trial. The next day, he called his second witness, a Dr. James Wilson, a medical researcher. Dr. Wilson was asked to describe the standard of research in the early 1940s, and not surprisingly, his testimony contrasted dramatically with that of our witness, Dr. Goldman. Dr. Wilson stated that animal studies were not really used very much during that period, and those he did mention tended to be experiments with monkeys rather than with rodents.

I didn't find this doctor very convincing, and I thought his opinion biased. Although Dr. Wilson said animal studies were not important, his own dissertation was on animal studies. He also admitted that he stopped using DES in 1966 as he was worried about its safety and because it was not effective. But what did the jury think? I studied the jurors' faces carefully, but I couldn't tell a thing. They were as inscrutable as ever.

The next witness was a Dr. Little, a large, middle-aged man with dark hair. He was a director of OB/GYN at Case Western Reserve School of Medicine. He seemed rather shy and he spoke so softly it

155

was often difficult to hear what he was saying. Justice Fraiman kept asking him to speak up. Dr. Little was another medical researcher and he had quite a lot to say. He testified to several points that had already been brought up as well as providing new ammunition for Beatie.

First of all, Beatie asked Dr. Little about the issue of whether the initial testing of DES was adequate. Dr. Little went over the process of the testing that was done by the Drs. Smith, the husband and wife team from Harvard whose studies on DES were used by Eli Lilly and the other drug companies to get the drug approved for use in pregnancy back in 1947. The Smiths were the researchers who used the historical controls instead of the double-blind controlled study that would have been so much more reliable. Dr. Little defended over and over again the work of the Smiths. He said their research had been highly competent, and reliable enough to provide the FDA with good reason to approve DES. It was difficult for me to understand on what basis Dr. Little was defending the Smith studies. It seemed that he was saying that the fact that they were from Harvard was in itself enough to make them reputable. They used a lot of people in their study, and he felt the Smiths were fine people. I was not convinced.

The next issue that Dr. Little addressed was the effectiveness of DES as a drug. Mr. Beatie seemed to feel that this was an important point. Dr. Little talked about the use of estrogens in pregnancy and how DES was effective. He stated that it was used to save pregnancies in women who otherwise would have miscarried. Mr. Beatie then asked him an extraordinary question. He asked Dr. Little if, in his expert opinion, he believed that had it not been for the DES that my mother had taken, I would not have been born. Without hesitation Dr. Little replied that he did not think that I would have been born had my mother not taken the DES.

My parents and I gasped in unison at this statement. Having heard Beatie's opening statement we knew it was coming, but it was hard to take anyway. Now the Lilly Company was trying to play God in making such a prediction. Beatie's point was that since I would not have been here at all if my mother had not taken DES, then it was irrelevant that I had suffered any damages because of it. I was disgusted. Dr. Little's testimony seemed contrary to everything I knew about DES, and I looked forward to Judge Finz's cross-examination of this witness. I had confidence that Finz would discredit his testimony.

Indeed, Judge Finz was masterful. He got up and walked over to Dr. Little sitting in the witness box. "Dr. Little," he said firmly. "Can you really sit there under oath and swear to this court that to the best of your professional knowledge had it not been for the DES Mrs. Bichler took, Joyce Bichler would not be here today? Can you, Dr. Little?"

Dr. Little looked uneasy. He glanced over at me and then back at Finz. "No, I can't say that."

There was a murmur of surprise throughout the courtroom. Dr. Little had clearly contradicted himself. My mother gripped my hand in anticipation of what else might come.

Judge Finz made Dr. Little repeat that he could not say absolutely that I wouldn't be here if it weren't for DES. Finz was in good form. He brought up the Dieckmann study of 1953, the first piece of research done on DES under controlled conditions. He announced to the court that this study clearly showed that DES was not effective in preventing miscarriage. In fact, the report statistics showed that bed rest alone was more effective.

Dr. Little acknowledged the Dieckmann study. He also acknowledged that the results of this study had been published and were known to the pharmaceutical world *before* DES had been given to my mother in mid-1953. Dr. Little then claimed that although he had been aware of the study at the time, he had still very much believed in DES. And, he said, he still believed in it.

Judge Finz asked Dr. Little if, even in the light of what we know about DES today, he would still give DES to pregnant women. Dr. Little looked straight at Judge Finz, and said, "Yes."

Judge Finz dramatically turned on his heel to face the jury. "I would like to point out to the court," he said, "that since 1971 DES has been banned by the FDA for use in pregnancy. Despite this," he continued, looking over at Dr. Little, "despite this, Dr. Little says he would still give the drug to pregnant women. I find that incredible."

The point was made and it was a good one.

Finz went on questioning Dr. Little. He pointed out that in the early 1960s the FDA itself had done effectiveness studies on various drugs. DES did not pass the test and received a failing grade. The drug companies were then told that they had to prove properly that DES was effective in preventing miscarriages. The drug companies were never able to produce adequate proof, yet here was Dr. Little still claiming DES was effective for such use, and basing his claim on the research done in the 1940s by the Drs. Smith.

And what about the Smiths? Why was Dr. Little defending their work so loyally like this? Judge Finz went over the doctor's credentials. He established that Dr. Little had in fact studied under the Smiths as a medical student and that he still had close ties with them, which seemed to make it difficult for him to evaluate their work from a dispassionate viewpoint. Having helped the Smiths with their work on DES, Dr. Little was also somewhat responsible for getting DES approved as a drug for pregnant women. His role in the whole affair was becoming very interesting.

Judge Finz asked Dr. Little to confirm that he had previously testified in another DES case (one that ended in a settlement just before the jury reached a verdict). Dr. Little said that was true. Judge Finz questioned him closely about this. "Is it true," Finz asked, "that you received a payment from Mr. Beatie to testify in that case?" (Getting paid a small compensation fee for time spent in the courtroom is not unusual.) There was another murmur from the onlookers. Dr. Little squirmed in his seat. Again he looked very uncomfortable and hesitated as he glanced over to where Mr. Beatie was sitting.

"No, I did not receive payment for my testimony in that case," he finally replied.

"Well, if you didn't receive the money," Judge Finz fired back, "who did?"

Dr. Little looked over at Beatie again. He seemed frightened as he answered. "The money went to the university where I work. A fund was set up for me in the name of the Smiths."

"Ah," said Finz, evidently pleased. "And how much money did Mr. Beatie give you for this fund?"

Dr. Little looked downward. "Twenty thousand dollars," he said softly.

Twenty thousand dollars? It was a staggering sum! Certainly it was a hefty amount of money to pay someone in exchange for testimony. Justice Fraiman had to ask for quiet as everyone whispered to each other in amazement. Judge Finz had finished with Dr. Little and he sat down. I looked over to see how Mr. Beatie had reacted to this brilliant piece of cross-examination. I could only see the back of Beatie's head but could tell that he was squirming in his chair.

I felt joyous. Dr. Little's testimony had probably helped us more than it hurt us. Mr. Beatie tried to repair the damage upon re-examination, but too much had been revealed.

That was one of the few days we went home feeling good. For once we chattered about the day's events as we drove back to West Nyack. Our spirits were lifted, our confidence was growing.

That night, just after dinner, Judge Finz called. He told me he had received a call from Mr. Beatie to say that Eli Lilly & Co. was ready to make a settlement offer of $100,000. My pulse quickened. Things were heating up now. But the amount was evidently more of a token gesture than a genuine statement of responsibility. Other women who had settled out of court had been offered more in the past. Finz told me that I should think about it carefully and call him back. He said it was entirely my decision, but he needed to know what I decided fairly soon. I promised to let him know as soon as I could, and thanked him.

I didn't want to alert my parents yet, so as discreetly as I could I asked Mike if he would come upstairs to discuss something.

Upstairs I told Mike what Judge Finz had just told me.

"Well, after what happened today, I'm not surprised," Mike said. "What do you think about it?"

"It's a lot of money to us," I said.

"Yes, but it's a settlement. As a settlement it's not a huge amount," Mike said. "*You* have to decide, Joyce, you know it's ultimately up to you."

There was no disagreement between us. We had discussed the possibility of offers in the past and decided that we wouldn't be bought off. We had all been through so much to get this far and I knew I had to see it through to the end. The trial was getting so much publicity now, this offer was more like hush money than a serious attempt to compensate me for my suffering. "No," I said, "we won't accept it. It's a lot of money, but we won't accept it."

Mike smiled and nodded in agreement. Neither of us had at any point been in this for the money, but as time had passed the principle of the matter had become increasingly important. We wanted to see Eli Lilly & Co.

admit that it was wrong, even if it meant turning down
an offer of more money than we had ever seen in our
lives. We knew it was a risk. We could still lose the case
and end up with nothing. But it was a risk we were
prepared to take. Mike and I hugged each other tight,
and I went downstairs and called Judge Finz back. He
accepted our decision.

The next morning we were all back in the courtroom.
Beatie was obviously surprised that we had turned
down his offer. I was glad that we could show him that
there were people who felt that there were things in this
world that were more important than money. At 10:00
A.M., just before the court session started, Mr. Beatie
strutted over to us. "Our offer is still good until noon,"
he said. "At that point it turns into a pumpkin." Evidently thinking he'd made a good joke, he went back to
his seat.

Mike and I repeated to Judge Finz that we were not
going to accept any offer. Finz was pleased. He wanted
to continue fighting as much as we did. Rather im-
pishly, he said that, come noon, he was going to call up
Beatie at his "command post" (the hotel room across
the street where the lawyers from Dewey, Ballantine
worked on my case around the clock) and say the same
thing that the American general, Anthony McAuliffe,
had said when surrounded at the Battle of the Bulge
and asked by the enemy to surrender: "Nuts." It
seemed appropriate enough for the occasion.

I shuddered when I saw who the next witness was to
be. It was Dr. Richart, a pathologist who worked in a
DES screening project in New York where DES-
exposed women were examined in the hope that any
signs of cancer would be spotted early. I had seen Dr.
Richart before, when Lilly had hired him to give me a
pretrial internal examination. Lilly had a right to have
me examined and this had been done several years earlier. In fact, Dr. Richart had examined me twice for

Lilly. At the time, I had liked him. He had seemed kind and sympathetic to both me and my mother, who had accompanied me. Yet here he was ready to testify against me. It was to be expected, I suppose, but I did feel exposed and betrayed yet again.

Dr. Richart took the stand. He now came across as a very different person from the one I remembered. He suddenly sounded pompous and arrogant. He was there to talk about the issue of cause and effect. He was going to talk about DES and my career. Dr. Richart stated that there was no absolute proof that DES caused cancer. It did not seem to matter to him that this particular cancer had not existed in young women before the advent of DES, that the Herbst Report had revealed that DES was the connecting link in women who had developed this type of cancer. Dr. Richart then went on to be more specific. He had, he said, examined my medical records and acknowledged that my cancerous lesion had rested partly on my vagina and cervix. Therefore, he said, he defined my cancer as cervical cancer. Next, with Mr. Beatie's assistance, Dr. Richart constructed a chart on a drawing board in front of the court. He said he was using Dr. Herbst's figures from recent studies and that they showed no relation between cervical cancer and DES.

Indeed, the finished chart made an impression on everyone. It showed no significant correlation between DES and cancer whatsoever.

Helped along by Beatie, Dr. Richart then said that he thought my cancer was not a result of the DES used by my mother at all. He said a proneness to cancer ran in the family, as shown by my father's illness. Beatie was still plugging at this point.

I was quite repulsed by Dr. Richart and by everything he said. What upset me most was that he was actually involved in the National DESAD Project, yet here he was denying that there was any direct link between DES and adenocarcinoma. It didn't make sense to me, particularly since the National DES Project had recently been publishing figures giving the percentages of women who got cancer from DES.

Judge Finz was going to cross-examine Dr. Richart after the recess. But while we all took a break, Finz and Mike had a good look at the chart Richart had drawn. Something was definitely wrong with it, especially since it had been drawn from Dr. Herbst's own figures. They looked at Dr. Herbst's article, from which the figures in the chart had been taken, and went over it step by step, reconstructing the chart that Beatie and Richart had drawn up. Before long, they discovered that there were some serious errors in the way the chart had been constructed. It had been drawn off-scale.

Suddenly everyone was returning to the courtroom. Judge Finz took his position to cross-examine Dr. Richart. He went over to the drawing board, set the first chart to one side and right next to it started another one, this time using the correct scale. He made Dr. Richart confirm that he was now in fact constructing the chart properly. Soon the chart was finished. Judge Finz had graphed exactly the same figures Dr. Richart had used, but now the result was strikingly different. In front of us all was a chart that showed that there certainly was a significant link between DES use and cancer. Dr. Richart now looked very foolish, and he became defensive and quite hostile to Judge Finz for the rest of the cross-examination. Eli Lilly had all the resources and funds at their fingertips. They called the top witnesses and experts and, once again, through the brilliant performance of our legal team, they were destroyed. Judge Finz was satisfied.

Mr. Beatie once again did his best to repair the damage but the point was clear for the jury to see. Richart kept saying that the incidence of cancer was still going up but DES use had leveled off. It would be up to the jurors now to make the final decision as to whom they believed and whether they thought my cancer was caused by diethylstilbestrol or not.

Dr. Richart's testimony left me with a very sick feeling. Here was a man who was supposedly helping DES daughters, yet who in effect was supporting the case of the drug companies that produced the drug. While taking state money to examine women for cancer caused by DES, he was testifying to the effect that no such link existed. It amazed me.

For the most part the trial was coming to a close. Publicity for the case had escalated even further. Most of the articles and news items were sympathetic and in their own way seemed to support our cause. I had become quite friendly with some of the reporters just from talking to them during the recesses, and the whole family had become used to spending many evenings talking to reporters over the telephone, having photographers come to the house to take pictures, and giving radio interviews. The word about DES was out. How far it spread would depend now on the outcome of the case—whether we won or we lost.

The cases had been presented for both sides. The last few days before the matter went into the hands of the jury were taken up by testimony from other witnesses and, finally, the closing arguments.

The closing arguments were very important. This trial had gone on for so many weeks, and so much highly technical information had been presented to the jury, that it was important to summarize the major points, bringing them all together again to refresh the jurors' memories.

Mr. Beatie was first to present his argument. Although what he had to say was fairly simple, it took him several hours to make all his points. His basic thesis was that, for the times, adequate testing had been done on DES and that had it not been for the drug, I would not have been born. He claimed, furthermore, that he had shown that DES does not cause cancer and that it certainly had not caused my cancer. Beatie went further still. He acknowledged my testimony and then, in a sickeningly "sympathetic" voice, talked about poor me, a young woman who had been so terribly injured. He said that it was so understandable that I wanted to take out my rage on somebody. He pointed out that during my testimony I had looked at him angrily. He said that I was angry at him, when *he* was certainly not responsible for what had occurred. Beatie was appealing to the deeply ingrained sexist attitudes held by so many people. By implying that I was an embittered and hysterical woman he was saying that I should not be taken seriously. It was a common ploy; men who fight for their rights are considered assertive and forceful, whereas women are seen as emotional and aggressive. Beatie was taking pains to create a picture of vengefulness and emotionality in what I was doing. It was a cheap trick but not, I suppose, unexpected.

Now it was Judge Finz's moment. He stood up and his force seemed to fill the room. He was fighting to the end. He began by emphasizing that in the 1940s DES was known to have the potential to cause harm to the fetus, yet it was never properly tested before being prescribed to pregnant women. He reiterated the point that by 1953, DES was known not to be effective in preventing miscarriage, yet it was left on the market. He repeated that DES had caused my cancer, that had the DES not acted as a trigger, I would not have developed this cancer. Judge Finz sounded quite lyrical as he used the analogy of rising steam. When someone draws up a bathtub full of steaming hot water, he said, if they are prudent they do not just jump into the tub without first testing the water with a finger or toe to see how hot it is. In the 1940s, Finz continued, the information on DES showed that the drug, like steaming hot water, had the potential for causing great harm. A prudent pharmaceutical company should have seen the steam rising and done proper animal tests before giving DES to pregnant women, thereby plunging them into the steaming bathwater, where they were scalded. The analogy was brilliant.

Judge Finz went on. He emphasized the significance of the drug companies having acted in concert to get DES approved and explained again why we were holding Eli Lilly & Co. responsible as the leading manufacturer of the drug. Then, as he talked again about my injuries, I remembered his eulogy on Truth. He did not dramatize or overemphasize anything. He simply described what had happened to me in a tone of honesty and genuine sympathy that left my eyes and many others' teary. It was the perfect approach.

Finz spoke for several hours. He built up to a crescendo of emotion. He was filled with feeling as he stood in front of the jury and said, "We are outraged at the tragedy of being victimized and used as [the pharmaceutical company's] human guinea pigs. Let us demand that the drugs being sold and put into the market for profit are effective and safe for human use.

"We cannot here alter the course of injustice that can be found right here even in the Bronx County. But we can here alter the course of this major injustice that has been perpetrated by this giant drug industry and be heard through the greatest power that we still here have in our democratic society, your voice as a juror.

"Few people, ladies and gentlemen, will ever be given the rare opportunity that you have in this case as independent and enlightened citizens. Few people in this world will ever have the opportunity in this lifetime, the opportunity that belongs to you today, that opportunity to say in this courtroom for everyone to hear, 'We are outraged at being used. We are outraged at being manipulated for profit. We are outraged at having been victimized and neglected with a lack of concern. We are people. We are human. Our lives are precious to us. Our lives count. Our health rights must be protected, and we are not going to permit this outrage to continue.'

"A little over a hundred years ago, a great president stood in a stilled battlefield on Pennsylvania soil and said, 'The world will little note nor long remember what we say here but can never forget what they did here.'

"This courtroom, ladies and gentlemen, is a battlefield. And this battle is one that truly pits the individual against the mighty. And let the women and men and children of our country, whose lives will surely be affected by the decision you will reach today, know that when history records your deeds it was done here by six proud, independent, courageous people in the Bronx. And let this be the step that links each of you with the progress of the future.

"We cannot expect to reach all of our goals and remove all injustice today. But today let us take the first step. Today, let us have courage. Today, let us demand that the standards be held high. Let us demand that those who commit wrongs upon us and our children and our children's children must be held accountable so that tomorrow and the tomorrows that come, there will be a world where safer drugs will be provided for our children and our children's children, free of the tragic consequences of careless acts and full of the assurance that the Joyce Bichler tragedy must never, never happen again in this nation."

By the time he had finished, he looked exhausted but satisfied. I could hardly contain my gratitude to him; he had outdone himself. As he sat down, I could sense that Mike, Mom, and Dad were all as excited as I was. Although I had sworn to myself that I would be cautious in this trial, I couldn't help feeling good. After Judge Finz's closing argument I couldn't see how anyone would go against us.

The jury would be given their charge the next day.

CHAPTER 14

The next morning we arrived at the courtroom early. I understood that the charging of the jury would take up a good part of the morning, but I was still very nervous because I knew that the deliberation would start that day anyway, after which the verdict could be reached at any time. I had butterflies in my stomach.

The charging of the jury began. The courtroom doors were closed. No one was allowed to go in or out. Justice Fraiman instructed the jurors on their duty and on how they were to proceed. We were anxious to see how he would put the questions to the jurors, but our fears were unfounded. Justice Fraiman was as stern and straightforward as ever. Justice Fraiman had composed the questions. There were seven questions the jurors had to answer:

1. Was DES reasonably safe for miscarriage purposes in 1953 (the year Joyce Bichler's mother was given DES for two or three weeks)?
2. Was DES a proximate cause of plaintiff's cancer?
3. In 1953, should a reasonably prudent drug manufacturer have foreseen that DES might cause cancer in the offspring of pregnant women who took it?
4. Foreseeing that DES might cause cancer in the offspring of pregnant women who took it, would a prudent drug manufacturer test it on pregnant mice before marketing it?
5. If DES had been tested on pregnant mice, would the tests have shown that DES caused cancer in their offspring?

168

6. Would a prudent manufacturer have marketed
   DES for miscarriage purposes in 1953 had it
   known that it caused cancer in the offspring of
   pregnant mice?
7. Did the defendent, Eli Lilly, and the other drug
   manufacturers act in concert with each other in
   the testing and marketing of DES for miscarriage
   purposes?

If I was to win this case, the jury had to come back
in my favor on each and every one of these questions.
If there was just one answer for the defendent, then the
jury would not have to go any further. The case would
be over and I would have lost. They were tough questions, and I shuddered as the jurors went off to the
deliberation room. Now came the waiting.

We had no idea at all how long the jury might be out.
That was the worst part of the waiting. The deliberation could take any length of time. The first hour or
two wasn't too bad, as I knew that no verdict would be
reached in that time, so I managed to relax and walk
around and talk to a number of friends there. But after
that, I became jittery. I didn't want to leave the courtroom, just in case. . . . I tried to read the newspaper,
but my powers of concentration were shot. Even when I
was talking to someone I jumped every time the door
opened or something in the old courtroom creaked. I
was so much on edge I was in agony.

Suddenly, Charlie the court clerk emerged from the
deliberation room and announced that the jury had sent
Justice Fraiman a note. Oh, my God, I thought, what
could that mean? My heart was getting more exercise,
pounding in my chest. I looked over at Judge Finz. He
seemed upset. He thought it was too soon. He knew
they couldn't have gone through all those questions in
this time. If they were through it had to mean that they
had answered against me on one of the early questions.
I felt a thud in my stomach. I sat down and grabbed

Mike's arm as we waited for Justice Fraiman to come in and read the note.

Justice Fraiman returned. He sat down and read the note. The foreman of the jury, it seemed, was requesting that a particular piece of evidence be brought in to them. I sighed with relief. So it wasn't over, not yet, but I didn't think my heart would be able to take much more of this.

We were still waiting by the end of the day. Still no word had been sent. Justice Fraiman called the attorneys into the court. Since it was clear that the jurors were not going to reach a verdict that day, Justice Fraiman suggested that they be sequestered overnight because there had been so much publicity surrounding the case. The attorneys agreed.

At about 5:00 P.M. the jurors were brought back into the courtroom and asked if they were close to reaching a decision. The foreman replied that they were making progress. Justice Fraiman then told them that he had arranged for them to spend the night at a Holiday Inn across the George Washington Bridge in New Jersey. He told them that it was highly unusual for a jury in a civil case to be sequestered, but owing to the importance of this case he felt that it was necessary. The jurors all looked very startled, and some tried to object. They certainly hadn't expected this to happen, and they weren't prepared for it. One juror even asked if she could at least go home to get her toothbrush. Justice Fraiman was firm with them. He said arrangements would be made to get some of their overnight belongings, and they could make calls to their families to tell them that they weren't coming home. None of the jurors seemed to like the idea. They discussed it among themselves for a few minutes and then told Justice Fraiman that they would like to deliberate for a little longer to see if they could make more progress before breaking for the night.

Justice Fraiman accepted their request and sent them

back in. We paced some more. I was very nervous that the jurors might now rush through to reach a verdict just so that they wouldn't have to sleep over. I was terrified that a practical problem like that might spoil everything. I prayed that that wouldn't happen.

It was now getting close to 7:00 P.M. The jurors were called back in and they said they were no closer to reaching a decision. They had obviously accepted that they weren't going home that night. Justice Fraiman instructed them that under no circumstances were they to discuss the case among themselves once they were out of the courtroom. The jurors were sent off for the night, and we went home, too, tired and weary. We all hoped that the next day would bring an end to all this.

The second day of deliberation. The jurors were back in their little room, and we had little to do except wait and pace. Dad had not come down with us for a few days as he hadn't been feeling well, but Arlene and her husband, Bob, were there every day now because their teaching jobs had ended for the summer. Dennis and Felice were now on their honeymoon, which had previously been delayed. They called us regularly from the Bahamas to see if any decision had been reached.

The hours dragged. This was the time for me to really get to know my attorneys. Judge Finz paced around the halls and frequently gave us his analysis of what he thought was going on in the deliberation room. I spent a lot of time with Sybil, when she wasn't taking care of various things that had to be done. I also talked to Ed and his wife, Sheila, who had started to come down regularly to the courtroom. In other circumstances it would have been good to sit and laugh and socialize, but there was too much tension now. Judge Finz, Sybil, and Ed had worked so hard and so long on this case and now there was nothing more to do except talk and worry. Mike and I did a lot of pacing together.

Suddenly Charlie was back again saying that the jury had sent a note to Justice Fraiman. Within a few minutes the jurors were back in the courtroom. Was this it? But no, the foreman had requested that the charge be read to them. They wanted to hear all the questions again. What did that mean? Was it good? Was it bad? Did it mean that they were close to the verdict? I was frantic with anticipation.

The charge was read to them again and then they were gone.

The minute the jurors had disappeared, the theories were flying. Judge Finz was confident; Beatie looked nervous; I just wasn't sure.

At noon we went out for lunch. I reluctantly left the courtroom and went with my family to the little delicatessen down the street. We had eaten there every day of the trial, eight weeks in a row, and I was sick of corned beef and pastrami. I couldn't eat a thing. Luckily Mom was so nervous about the jury that she either didn't notice or else she didn't think it appropriate to remind me just then of my promise to eat properly.

Back to the courtroom. Soon after lunch another note came from the jurors. Justice Fraiman came out again to read the note. "We are hopelessly deadlocked."

I thought I was going to pass out. Up until then I had believed that this trial could end in only one of two ways: Either we would win or else we would lose. Either way it would be over. But now I saw that there was another alternative, one that was worse than losing: It could end in a mistrial. That would mean we would have to start all over again. I couldn't handle that in any way. I sat there in shock when I realized what could happen. I turned to look at my family. They were having the same thoughts and were as shocked as I was. It couldn't happen. It *couldn't*.

Justice Fraiman called the jurors out into the courtroom. He questioned the foreman of the jury, who repeated that they were deadlocked. Justice Fraiman told him that it was important to try to reach a decision if possible. He asked them to continue deliberating for the rest of the afternoon, at the end of which, he said, he would call them out again to see if they were any nearer a decision.

The jury left and throughout the rest of the day kept asking for other specific pieces of evidence. They were examining everything very carefully.

I was beginning to feel worn down. Why can't this just end? I kept asking myself. Why can't we go back to our normal existence? I felt as though any strength I had left was being sapped from me. I had a strong desire to collapse in a heap and weep my heart out. But I didn't.

In the late afternoon Justice Fraiman called the jury back again and asked them about whether they thought it was worth pursuing the deliberations. The foreman replied that they had made some progress and that they would like to continue tomorrow. Fraiman looked relieved. We were relieved. And the jurors were relieved, for they were allowed to go to their own homes under strict orders not to discuss the case or react or listen to any publicity regarding it.

Thank goodness it was back again tomorrow, but was it never going to end?

The third day of deliberation. The jury was very active. They asked for much of the testimony to be read back to them—particular Dr. Hines' and Dr. Krumholz's testimonies. The attorneys took turns reading the requested evidence to the jury. It took hours and hours. I was becoming very impressed by the dedication and endurance of this jury. They seemed determined to reach the right decision even if it meant having the entire trial read back to them.

The jury went back into the deliberation room and we were all left to wait again. I was beginning to feel a little crazy, but I wasn't the only one. In the hallway there was sporadic laughter from people for no reason at all. Everyone was so tense that laughter was the only release we had.

It was the end of day again. The jury foreman told Justice Fraiman that progress was still being made and that they wanted to continue the next day. I was anguished. No one had ever heard of a civil jury deliberating this long. It was incredible, but at least we hadn't lost yet.

The fourth day of deliberation. It was Friday, the end of the week. We knew that Justice Fraiman might end the case today; he couldn't let it drag on forever. The jurors knew this too. Justice Fraiman told the jurors he would not hold them beyond the end of the day. He said he did not intend to hold them captive until they reached a verdict. They had to reach a decision by late that afternoon or a mistrial might be declared. Judge Finz said he was of the mind to have it end in a mistrial rather than lose. He was preparing us to be ready for this to happen today. I was despondent but readier to accept a mistrial if it had to come.

More evidence was examined by the jury. More deliberations. Then, in the middle of the afternoon, Charlie the court clerk suddenly came scurrying around the courtroom looking for Justice Fraiman. There was so much activity, I thought the jury must have reached a decision. Everyone was trying to find out what was happening. My heart was racing again. But then someone said that one of the women jurors had become ill. One person said it was a heart attack, another said she had passed out. No one really knew. There was total confusion in the courtroom. Everyone was excited. What was going on? No one seemed to know.

After a long time, someone said that the ill juror had been taken over to a doctor across from the courthouse and that she would be all right. It seemed certain now that the trial would be over, but we heard nothing more for a while.

The attorneys for both sides were called into the judge's chambers. Judge Finz and Beatie went off together. The rest of us were left to pace the courtroom. This was the end. We could only wait for the word. But no one wanted to believe it.

Finally, the door to the judge's chambers opened and out walked Judge Finz and Beatie, both, to my astonishment, looked rather giggly. Finz started to do a Groucho Marx impression. I thought they had both finally cracked under the pressures. The attorneys tried to compose themselves, and Judge Finz then took us to a side of the courtroom to explain what had happened.

Juror number two had become ill. She had some indigestion but was now all right. She had now come back from the doctor, who said that her health wasn't in danger and he had given her medication for her high blood pressure. Justice Fraiman had wanted to talk to her with both attorneys present to ask her directly if she wanted to continue. He felt that if the tension were too much for her, she should have the option to call it quits. But when they all went into the room where the juror was, they found her asleep. The medication the doctor had given her had made her drowsy.

That was the state of play at that point. It was farcical. Finz and Beatie knew that the juror's illness was hardly a laughing matter but the tension was so great they had just broken down. So there we were, late on a Friday afternoon, after eight weeks of trial and four days of deliberations, and nobody knew what to do, while the juror slept!

Justice Fraiman called the attorneys back to his chambers to discuss the situation. It was decided that he would call the remaining five jurors back into the courtroom, ask them what they wanted to do, and go from there.

The others were called back in. They were told about number two's condition and it was explained that she was going to be all right. Justice Fraiman asked if they would like to continue their deliberations on Monday, provided that number two (when she was able to respond) said that she would also be willing to continue. Each juror answered quickly and confidently. Each said yes. Justice Fraiman told them that if they were to continue, they were not to be influenced by number two's illness. He then asked each juror again if her or she could continue without having that be an influencing factor. All the jurors said that they certainly would not let that be a factor.

The jury was dismissed. Juror number two was escorted home to rest for the weekend. I felt I was hanging in mid-air. I could not believe that the trial was going to continue into the next week. We had all been so ready for it to end today. Now this awful agony would be prolonged. The hardest part was that we couldn't even be sure that juror number two would want to continue. After what had happened, who would blame her if she decided she didn't want to push herself? We could suffer over the weekend, to come into the courtroom on Monday and find that number two had decided not to continue—and the trial would be over. Not knowing was very painful.

All the same, I was encouraged. The other five jurors seemed to feel so strongly that they wanted to continue, that they wanted to reach a verdict. I kept thinking that if they were against us and it seemed likely that the verdict would be in Lilly's favor, would they then be pushing so strongly to come up with a decision against me? I couldn't believe that these people, who seemed so committed to do the right thing, would feel so strongly against me that they would fight to bring in a negative verdict. I felt they must be with me. It seemed more logical that they would want to do something positive rather than something negative. For the first time in days I allowed a tiny bit of hope to creep in. Now everything depended on juror number two.

The weekend hours seemed to crawl by. There was absolutely nothing I could do to take my mind off the trial. At this point there was nothing else in the world except DES and the trial. Nothing. San Francisco and work seemed a universe away. There was only the trial, and it was making me a crazy person.

Late on Saturday night, Judge Finz called. Obviously Lilly was having the same feeling that I was and Beatie had contacted Finz to tell him that their previous offer still stood. He said I had until Monday morning to respond. Finz still said it was entirely up to me to decide.

I told him I would have to think about it and call him back. Again I discussed it with Mike. In situations as tense as this trial had been, relationships are either strengthened or broken apart. Ours was certainly strengthened. While we were crabby and touchy with everyone else around us, we somehow managed to keep calm with each other. Throughout the past eight weeks we had felt closer than ever. Perhaps it was a matter of survival. Mike was totally opposed to accepting the offer, not only for the old reasons but also because he, the eternal optimist, was convinced that the jury was with us. He was also sure that number two would continue on Monday. I wasn't so sure at all. The idea of a mistrial appalled me, but I knew it was very possible now. At the same time, we knew that if we accepted this offer of $100,000 we would never know what the outcome would have been. To end right here would mean that there would be no Monday, no outcome. The trial would be over and for the rest of our lives we would wonder what would have happened if we had continued. We agreed we could not live with that. We had to take the risk. We would be prepared for the defeat if it came, and we would go through the fight again if a mistrial were called. The one small chance of winning made it necessary for us to continue. Again I knew I would not be stopped by such an offer. If Eli Lilly & Co. were willing to make an offer that reflected an acknowledgment of their responsibility to the DES-exposed, then matters would be different. But this sum was truly negligible to them, even though it was quite enough to keep Mike and me financially well off for a long time. No, our principles were too important, we decided.

On Sunday morning, I called Judge Finz back and told him our decision. He accepted it and said he would see us in court on Monday. But when my mother heard what we had done, she could not believe it. She was pessimistic about the outcome and didn't want us to come out of it all with nothing. She said we were being too idealistic and very foolish. Mom was very upset. She said that if it were a mistrial, neither she nor my father could go through it all. I would be on my own. I didn't like to hear that, but I could understand my parents' feelings. My sister, Arlene, also evidently thought we were crazy, though she was tactful about it.

Mike and I were alone in our decision. Perhaps we were crazy, perhaps my family was right. But we knew that we had to see this thing through. We reasoned that even if we lost, others would still be able to continue the battle and try to win against the drug companies— we wouldn't have jeopardized their chances. But if we won, then it would help others tremendously. We were so close to winning, we couldn't give up at this point. We had started out with no money and if we lost the case, we would not miss the money we hadn't won. At least we would have stuck to our principles and would know that Eli Lilly & Co. couldn't buy us off. Come Monday morning I could look into Mr. Beatie's eyes and not feel compromised.

* * *

Monday morning eventually did come. No one yet knew whether juror number two was going to show up or not that morning. Mike and I took a private stroll around the courthouse hallway. As we turned a corner, an elevator door opened up, and there was number two! Not only was she there but she practically burst out from the elevator, looking healthier than either Mike or I at the moment. She strode down the hallway and disappeared into the jury room. She was here!

Within a few minutes the court had convened. Justice Fraiman questioned number two on how she felt. She said she was just fine. Justice Fraiman again emphasized to the jurors that they should not be influenced by Friday's incident and they all agreed again that they wanted to continue. Off they went to the deliberation room, and again we were left to wait.

The agony was acute. The waiting was more difficult than ever. Reporters were swarming all around the courtroom. Waiting. Waiting.

It was lunchtime. Everyone went out to lunch. I didn't go. I couldn't leave the courtroom. I needed to stay close by. Mike stayed with me. Arlene brought me back a milkshake to keep up my strength. I couldn't drink it.

About forty-five minutes after lunch, Ed and Mike persuaded me to take a stroll. We were at the far end of the hallway, looking down to the courtroom door, when suddenly the swinging door opened and Arlene shoved her head out. "This is it," she called excitedly. "The jury's coming in!"

I jumped with fright. Mike started pulling me down the hallway to the courtroom. I felt nauseous. This is it, this is it, this is it. My heart beat frantically in time with my thoughts.

I took my seat between Mike and Mom. Both took my hand. I was shaking all over. Dad was here today. He knew it was an important day to be present. The

179

jurors came in and took their seats. No one smiled. No one looked glum. No one shook a head.

Justice Fraiman appeared. He asked the foreman if they had reached a verdict. The foreman replied that they had. My stomach felt knotted. I took a deep breath. Fraiman read the first question. "Was DES safe for miscarriage purposes in 1953?"

The foreman looked at the notes he had in front of him. He looked up and said, "No. 5–1."

It was like a hammer striking. Okay, one for us.

Justice Fraiman continued. "Did DES cause Joyce Bichler's vaginal and cervical cancer?"

The foreman paused. "Yes," he finally said, "5, with one abstention."

Tears started to roll down my cheeks.

"In 1953 should a reasonably prudent drug manufacturer have foreseen that DES might cause cancer in the offspring of pregnant women who took it?"

There was a long pause. This was the most difficult question. "Yes, 6–0."

Judge Finz pounded with joy on the table in front of him. We squeezed each other's hands. This was it. We had cleared the hurdle.

"Foreseeing that DES might cause cancer in the offspring of pregnant women who took it, would a prudent drug manufacturer have tested it on pregnant mice before marketing it?"

"Yes. 6–0."

"If DES had been tested on pregnant mice, would the tests have shown that DES caused cancer in their offspring?"

"Yes, 6–0."

I was sobbing so hard I could hardly hear.

"Would a prudent manufacturer have marketed DES for miscarriage purposes in 1953 had it known that it caused cancer in the offspring of pregnant mice?"

"No. 6–0."

"Did the defendant, Eli Lilly, and the other drug

manufacturers, act in concert with each other in the testing and marketing of DES for miscarriage purposes?"

This was also an important, landmark question.

"Yes. 6–0."

"How much do you award Ms. Bichler?"

There was no hesitation. "$500,000."

Suddenly most of the jurors were smiling. Mike and I jumped to our feet. We hugged. We were both crying. Mom and Dad hugged me too and then hugged Mike. There was pandemonium in the courtroom. Shouting and cheering and whistling. Judge Finz ran over to me and we embraced. It was the moment of my life. I had won. I had survived.

APPENDIX 1*

DES (diethylstilbestrol) is a synthetic female hormone (estrogen) that was used to prevent miscarriages. It is estimated that between 1941 and 1971, several million women were given this drug during pregnancy, especially if they had a history of previous miscarriage or slight bleeding, or had diabetes.

Between 60 and 90 percent of daughters born to women who took DES during their pregnancies have been found to have changes in their vagina or cervix due to their DES exposure. The most common change is called adenosis. This is the presence of a type of glandular tissue in the vagina that usually occurs in the cervix. This is a benign change and believed not to be dangerous although it does need to be monitored by a doctor or health professional.

In some DES daughters the vagina and cervix as well as uterus show structural changes. Although these changes do not necessarily interfere with reproductive functions, it has recently been found that with some DES daughters there is a greater chance of difficulty during pregnancy (both in terms of becoming pregnant or carrying a pregnancy to term) than with non-DES daughters. These problems are related to the DES-caused changes in the cervix (incompetent cervix) as well as changes in the uterus (T-shaped uterus). But many DES daughters have had normal pregnancies and healthy babies.

* Most of the following information was taken directly from *You May Be a DES Daughter* and *You May Be a DES Son*. Both pamphlets are available from DES Action (See Appendix 3 for addresses).

Approximately one in one thousand DES daughters will develop cancer. This cancer (clear cell adenocarcinoma) usually starts on the cervix or vagina. The age range for developing this cancer is from seven to thirty-one, with most cases being found in the late teens. In many cases this cancer is symptomless and is discovered when the proper DES screening tests are done. If found early, this cancer can be treated.

It is vitally important to find out if you are DES-exposed. Many DES mothers, daughters, and sons do not know they were exposed to this harmful drug. Your mother may not remember taking DES or may not know what kind of medication she took while pregnant. To find out whether you were exposed, ask your mother if she had any of these problems during pregnancy:

- Did she have bleeding, miscarriages, premature births, or diabetes?
- Did she take any hormones during the first five months of pregnancy?
- Can her medical records (doctor, hospital) be checked to see if she took DES?

If there is any reason at all to believe that your mother may have taken DES (or if you can't find out and just want to be sure), go to a doctor or clinic with experience in DES screening. The time to go is:

- After you have started your first period, or
- If you are fourteen years old or over, or
- If you have any unusual vaginal discharge or irregular bleeding.

DES-caused changes may not show up in the usual pelvic examination or Pap smears given by most doctors. The exam consists of:

- A careful inspection of the vagina and cervix for physical differences.

- A gentle palpation of the walls of the vagina.
- A four-sided (quadrant) Pap test, where the walls of the vagina are lightly scraped to get cells for laboratory inspection under a microscope.
- Iodine staining of the vagina and cervix (normal tissue stains brown, adenosis tissue does not stain).

Depending on the results of these tests you may need some further tests done. These include:

- Looking at the tissue of the vagina with a colposcope (special binoculars that magnify tissue). Photographs of abnormal tissue can be taken and changes can be watched over a period of time.
- Taking tiny samples of tissue from the vagina by biopsy. The tissue is sent to a laboratory and examined under a microscope.

If the above procedures detect changes, you may be asked to return every three to six months for repeat examinations. It is important that you receive regular follow-up examinations and that you feel comfortable with the health care you are receiving.

If you know you are a DES daughter, you should also know that taking any estrogen (in pills or injections) may be harmful. Estrogen is contained in most birth control pills and morning-after pills. Studies are underway to determine whether birth control pills increase the cancer risk of DES daughters. Many physicians believe that DES daughters should use other contraceptive methods.

It is not only DES daughters who are affected. DES sons have also been found to have changes related to their DES exposure. DES sons face an increased chance of having fertility problems and testicular abnormalities. Studies have shown that DES sons have more sperm and semen abnormalities than men who have not been exposed to DES. About 30 percent of DES sons have some type of testicular abnormality. The most common is benign (not cancerous) cysts in the epididymus. The epididymus is the collecting structure in the back of each testicle where mature sperm is stored. These cysts are painless growths that feel like small lumps. They may disappear and then recur over time.

Extremely small testes and undescended testes are other common DES-related changes. Men with undescended testes (even if their mothers did not take DES) have an increased chance of developing testicular cancer.

If you think you are a DES son, first go to a urologist for an examination. Second, get in the habit of self-examination of the testes.

As far as the mothers themselves, recent studies suggest a possible increase in breast cancer and cancer of the uterus, cervix, or ovaries. DES mothers are encouraged to have regular gynecological and breast examinations and should practice breast self-examination every month. Before taking any estrogens, such as birth control pills, the morning-after pill, or estrogens for menopausal symptoms, DES mothers should discuss the benefits and risks with their doctor. Taking more estrogen in any of these forms may add to the risk of cancer.

In a sense, all of us have been medicated with DES. For many years now, DES has been used in cattle feed to increase cattle weight before slaughter. There have been traces of DES found in the beef that we eat, particularly in organ meats like beef liver. As of November 1979, DES for this use has been banned by the Food and Drug Administration, but unfortunately there have been reports of many violations of this order.

Because most DES daughters are in the seventeen-to-thirty-five-year age group, the long-term risks of other forms of cancer are not yet known. That is why it is important for the DES-exposed to continue their follow-up examinations for the rest of their lives. In addition women should practice breast self-examination every month.

For more information regarding DES exposure or where to go for the special health screening, contact the OB/GYN department of the nearest medical school and ask if they have a clinic or can refer you to a doctor or clinic in your area. You can also get more information from a DES Action group listed in Appendix 3.

APPENDIX 2:
DES Time Line

1938: DES synthesized by Sir Charles Dodds in England.

1942: United States pharmaceutical companies get DES approved for use with menopausal women, to prevent lactation, for treatment of breast cancer, and for treatment of prostate cancer.

1941–1947: Uncontrolled tests done on human subjects by Drs. George and Olive Smith and Priscilla White with DES. No tests done at this time on pregnant animals to see the effects of DES on their offspring.

1947: Food and Drug Administration approves DES for use during pregnancy.

1950–1970: DES hailed as "wonder drug." DES given (often mixed with vitamins) to millions of women to "help" with their pregnancies.

1953: First controlled study of DES (Dieckmann study) shows conclusively that DES is totally ineffective in preventing miscarriage. Statistical analysis of study shows that bed rest alone was more effective than DES. DES continues to be given to pregnant women.

1962: FDA gives DES a failing grade for effectiveness.

1971: Dr. Arthur Herbst publishes a paper in the *New England Journal of Medicine* connecting a rare form of vaginal cancer in young women with *in utero* exposure to DES.

1972: Other effects of DES in young women found.

1972: FDA bans use of DES during pregnancy. The drug remains on the market for its many other uses

—menopausal hormone replacement, morning-after pill, etc.

1972–1980: Continued research finds other effects of DES exposure, including fertility problems in both daughters and sons, a slight increase in breast cancer in mothers, structural changes in sex organs of daughters and sons.

1978: Federal DES Task Force convenes. Some of the recommendations are that DES daughters should avoid use of the birth control pill and that further research should be done on the effects of DES.

1979: Joyce Bichler is the first DES daughter to win a lawsuit against a pharmaceutical company that produced DES. A New York jury found that insufficient testing was done on this drug before it was marketed. Eli Lilly & Co. appeals the court's decision.

1979: DES banned by the FDA for use in cattle feed.

1980: DES continues to be on the market. Many DES-exposed continue to be unaware of their special health needs. New cases of DES-related cancer continue to be reported. Research continues on the long-term risks of DES exposure. Premature births related to DES exposure continue to affect the next generation of the DES-exposed.

1981: A New York State Appeals Court unanimously upholds the jury verdict against Eli Lilly & Company awarding Joyce Bichler $500,000 in damages.

APPENDIX 3:
Listing of DES Action Groups

DES Action, National

East Coast Office:

Long Island Jewish-
Hillside Medical Center
New Hyde Park, NY 11040

West Coast Office:

1638 B Haight St.
San Francisco, CA
94117

Local DES Action Groups

DES Action/Connecticut
P.O. Box 49
Mansfield Depot, CT 06251

DES Action/Detroit
Jan Loveland
P.O. Box 8663
Detroit, MI 48224

DES Action/Florida
Joan Grenoble
9586 Portside Dr.
Seminole, FL 33542

DES Action/Lansing
P.O. Box 66
East Lansing, MI 48823

DES Action/Massachusetts
P.O. Box 126
Stoughton, MA 02070

DES Action/Minnesota
1130 Nicollet Mall
Minneapolis, MN 55403

DES Action/Great Lakes
626 Twelfth Avenue
Two Harbors, MN 55616

DES Action/New Jersey
P.O. Box 323
Westwood, NJ 07675

DES Action/New York
Long Island Jewish-Hillside
Medical Center
New Hyde Park, NY 11040

DES Action/Oregon
P.O. Box 12092
Portland, OR 97212

DES Action/Sacramento
c/o YMCA
1122 17th St.
Sacramento, CA 95811

DES Action/San Francisco
1638 B Haight St.
San Francisco, CA 94117

DES Action/Washington
P.O. Box 5311
Rockville, MD 20851

APPENDIX 4: Names Under Which DES Has Been Sold

Amperone
AVC cream with Dienestrol
Benzestrol
Chlorotrianisene
Comestrol
Cyren A
Cyren B
Delvinal
DES
DesPlex
Di-Erone
Diestryl
Dibestil
Dienestrol
Dienestrol cream
Dienoestrol
Diethylstilbestrol Dipalmitate
Diethylstilbestrol Diphosphate
Diethylstilbestrol Dipropionate
Diethylstilbenediol

Digestil
Domestrol
Estan
Estilben
Estrobene
Estrobene DP
Estrosyn
Fonatol
Gynben
Gyneben
Hexestrol
Hexoestrol
H-Bestrol
Menocrin
Meprane
Mestilbol
Methallenestril
Metystil
Microest
Mikarol
Mikarol forti
Milestrol
Monomestrol
Neo-Oestranol I

Neo-Oestranol II
Nulabort
Oestrogenine
Oestromenin
Oestromon
Orestol
Pabestrol D
Palestrol
Progravidium
Restrol
Stil-Rol
Stilbal
Stilbestrol
Stilbestronate
Stilbetin
Stilbinol
Stilboestroform

Stilboestrol
Stilboestrol DP
Stilestrate
Stilpalmiate
Stilphostrol
Stilronate
Stilrone
Stils
Synestrin
Synestrol
Synthoestrin
Tace
Teserene
Tylandril
Tylosterone
Vallestril
Willestrol

APPENDIX 5:
General Readings
on DES

"DES Action/Voice," a quarterly newsletter available from DES Action/National, at Long Island Jewish-Hillside Medical Center; New Hyde Park, NY 11040.

Epstein, Samuel. *The Politics of Cancer.* San Francisco: Sierra Club Books, 1978.

From One Teen-ager to Another, a pamphlet available from DES Action/National.

HEW Task Force Report on DES, available from the National Cancer Institute Hotline (free), 1-800-638-6694.

Seaman, Barbara, and Seaman, Gideon. *Woman and the Crisis in Sex Hormones.* New York: Rawson Publishing Co., 1977.

You May Be a DES Daughter, a pamphlet available from DES Action/National.

You May Be a DES Son, a pamphlet available from DES Action/National.